THE SIMPLE MEDITERRANEAN DIET
COOKBOOK FOR BEGINNERS:

1800+ Days of Tasty and Easy Recipes for Everyday Healthy Living . Includes 30-day meal plan

LINETTE JOHNSTON

THE SIMPLE MEDITERRANEAN DIET COOKBOOK FOR BEGINNERS:

1800+ Days of Tasty and Easy Recipes for Everyday Healthy Living . Includes 30-day meal plan

Copyright © 2024 Linette Johnston.
All rights reserved.

No part of this publication may be reproduced, distributed, or transmitted in any form or by any means, including photocopying, recording, or other electronic or mechanical methods, without the prior written permission of the author, except in the case of brief quotations embodied in critical reviews and certain other noncommercial uses permitted by copyright law. For permission requests, write to the author at the address below:

Linette Johnston

Disclaimer

The information provided in this cookbook, "The Simple Mediterranean Diet Cookbook for Beginners," is intended for educational purposes only. It is not intended as a substitute for professional medical advice, diagnosis, or treatment. Always seek the advice of your physician or other qualified health provider with any questions you may have regarding a medical condition. Never disregard professional medical advice or delay in seeking it because of something you have read in this book.

The author and publisher of this book are not responsible for any adverse effects or consequences resulting from the use of any recipes, suggestions, or procedures described in this book. The dietary and nutritional information provided in this book are based on the author's research, knowledge, and personal experience with the Mediterranean diet. Individual results may vary.

The author and publisher make no representations or warranties of any kind with respect to the accuracy, applicability, fitness, or completeness of the contents of this book. The information contained in this book is strictly for educational purposes. If you wish to apply ideas contained in this book, you take full responsibility for your actions.

TABLE OF CONTENT

INTRODUCTION 7

CHAPTER 1. LIFESTYLE ADVICE 8

CHAPTER 2. BREAKFAST 10

Avocado Toast with Cherry Tomatoes 10
Shakshuka (Poached Eggs
in Tomato Sauce) 10
Mediterranean Breakfast Bowl 11
Spinach and Feta Frittata 11
Quinoa Breakfast Porridge 12
Mediterranean Omelette
with Sun-Dried Tomatoes 12
Hummus Toast with Cucumbers
and Radishes 13
Whole Wheat Pancakes
with Fresh Berries 13
Mediterranean Breakfast Tacos 14
Mediterranean Smoothie Bowl 14
Herbed Goat Cheese
and Vegetable Muffins 15
Lemon Ricotta Pancakes 15
Egg and Veggie Breakfast Wrap 16
Feta and Spinach Muffins 16
Millet Porridge with Nuts and Fruits 17
Tofu Scramble with Mediterranean
Veggies 17

CHAPTER 3. SALADS 18

Mediterranean Chickpea Salad 18
Spinach Salad with Pomegranate
and Walnuts 18
Tabbouleh with Fresh Herbs
and Lemon 19
Greek Salad with Feta
and Olives 19

Warm Farro Salad with Roasted
Vegetables 20
Beet and Orange Salad with Goat
Cheese 20
Roasted Red Pepper and Chickpea
Salad 21
Avocado and Shrimp Salad 21
Kale Salad with Lemon and Garlic 22
Tomato and Mozzarella Salad with Basil .. 22
Zucchini Noodle Salad with Pesto 23
White Bean and Tuna Salad 23
Caprese Salad with Balsamic Reduction ... 24
Quinoa and Black Bean Salad 24
Roasted Cauliflower and Chickpea Salad .. 25
Cucumber and Tomato Salad with Feta ... 25
Fennel and Orange Salad 26
Orzo Salad with Kalamata Olives 26

CHAPTER 4. MEAT AND POULTRY 27

Mediterranean Meatballs
in Tomato Sauce 27
Braised Lamb with Apricots 27
Chicken Shawarma with Tahini Sauce ... 28
Stuffed Peppers with Ground Turkey ... 28
Chicken Cacciatore 29
Chicken Tagine with Olives
and Lemons 29
Beef and Mushroom Stew 30
Herbed Turkey Meatloaf 30
Beef and Eggplant Casserole 31
Mediterranean Beef and Lentil Stew 31
Lamb Kebabs with Mint Yogurt Sauce ... 32
Greek Lemon Chicken 32
Chicken and Artichoke Casserole 33
Chicken and Vegetable Skewers 33
Grilled Chicken with Avocado Salsa 34

Honey Mustard Chicken Thighs 34
Lamb Kofta 35
Beef and Mushroom Stroganoff 35

CHAPTER 5. FISH AND SEAFOOD 36

Baked Salmon with Dill and Lemon 36
Shrimp Scampi with Garlic and Olive Oil 36
Grilled Swordfish with Capers 37
Garlic Butter Shrimp with Zoodles 37
Grilled Octopus with Lemon and Olive Oil 38
Mediterranean Mussels in White Wine Sauce 38
Pan-Seared Scallops with Herb Butter . . . 39
Seafood Risotto with Saffron 39
Grilled Shrimp with Mango Salsa 40
Baked Tilapia with Spinach and Feta 40
Grilled Mackerel with Citrus Salsa 41
Seared Tuna with Sesame and Soy 41
Grilled Calamari with Lemon and Parsley 42
Roasted Sea Bass with Olives and Tomatoes 42

CHAPTER 6. VEGETABLES AND SIDES 43

Roasted Eggplant with Tahini 43
Grilled Zucchini with Lemon and Basil . . . 43
Baked Feta with Tomatoes and Olives . . . 44
Ratatouille 44
Mediterranean Mashed Potatoes 45
Grilled Asparagus with Parmesan 45
Stuffed Mushrooms with Spinach and Feta 46
Roasted Butternut Squash with Sage 46
Baked Zucchini Chips 47
Mediterranean Quinoa Stuffed Tomatoes 47
Roasted Beet Salad with Feta 48

Stuffed Acorn Squash with Wild Rice 48
Roasted Fennel with Parmesan 49
Baked Stuffed Eggplant Rolls 49

CHAPTER 7. VEGETARIAN MAINS 50

Eggplant Parmesan 50
Spinach and Ricotta Stuffed Peppers 50
Chickpea and Spinach Stew 51
Mediterranean Vegetable Stir-Fry 51
Lentil and Vegetable Shepherd's Pie 52
Stuffed Acorn Squash with Quinoa 52
Vegetable Paella 53
Greek Style Lentil Soup 53
Mediterranean Vegetable Casserole 54
Sweet Potato and Black Bean Enchiladas 54
Grilled Vegetable Skewers 55
Eggplant and Tomato Bake 55
Chickpea and Vegetable Tagine 56
Greek Style Stuffed Zucchini 56
Tofu and Vegetable Stir-Fry 57
Roasted Garlic and Herb Cauliflower Steaks 57

CHAPTER 8. SNACKS AND APPETIZERS 58

Hummus with Pita Chips 58
Spanakopita Triangles 58
Marinated Olives 59
Falafel with Tzatziki 59
Feta Stuffed Dates 60
Mediterranean Bruschetta 60
Lemon and Herb Marinated Feta 61
Zucchini Fritters 61
Garlic Shrimp Skewers 62
Stuffed Grape Leaves 62
Sun-Dried Tomato Tapenade 63
Smoked Salmon Crostini 63
Greek Yogurt Dip with Fresh Veggies 64

Roasted Eggplant Dip 64
Cheese and Olive Platter 65
Pita Chips with Lemon Garlic Hummus 65

CHAPTER 9. PASTA 66

Spaghetti Aglio e Olio 66
Lemon and Artichoke Penne 66
Shrimp and Feta Linguine 67
Greek Style Stuffed Shells 67
Pasta with Anchovy Sauce 68
Lemon and Garlic Shrimp Pasta 68
Fettuccine with Roasted Tomatoes 69
Penne Arrabbiata with Olives 69
Tomato and Basil Penne 70
Whole Wheat Spaghetti with Clams 70
Pesto and Sun-Dried Tomato Penne 71
Ricotta and Spinach Stuffed Manicotti . . . 71
Caprese Pasta with Fresh Basil 72
Chickpea Pasta with Garlic and Parsley . . 72
Zucchini Noodles with Marinara 73
Pappardelle with Mushroom Ragu 73

CHAPTER 10. PIZZAZ, WRAPS, AND SANDWICHES 74

Mediterranean Veggie Pizza 74
Greek Gyro Wraps 74
Hummus and Veggie Wraps 75
Caprese Sandwich 75
Falafel Pita 76
Grilled Chicken Pesto Panini 76
Mediterranean Tuna Wrap 77
Shrimp and Avocado Sandwich 77
Roasted Veggie Pita 78
Greek Salad Pizza 78
Turkey and Hummus Wrap 79
Spinach and Feta Flatbread 79
Lamb Gyro 80
Grilled Halloumi Wrap 80

Italian Sub with Olive Tapenade 81
Roasted Beet and Goat Cheese Sandwich 81
Mediterranean Turkey Club 82
Hummus and Roasted Red Pepper Sandwich 82
Portobello Mushroom Burger 83
Smoked Salmon Bagel with Cream Cheese 83

CHAPTER 11. BEANS AND GRAINS 84

Quinoa Tabbouleh 84
Lentil and Vegetable Stew 84
Chickpea and Spinach Curry 85
Farro Salad with Roasted Vegetables 85
White Bean and Kale Soup 86
Mediterranean Barley Risotto 86
Bulgur Wheat Salad 87
Brown Rice Pilaf with Vegetables 87
Red Lentil Soup with Lemon 88
Black Bean and Corn Salad 88
White Bean and Spinach Stew 89
Mediterranean Spelt Salad 89
Three-Bean Salad with Lemon Vinaigrette 90
Red Lentil and Spinach Dhal 90
Mediterranean Bulgur Pilaf 91
Rice and Bean Stuffed Peppers 91

CHAPTER 12. STAPLES, SAUCES, DIPS, AND DRESSINGS 92

Tzatziki Sauce 92
Harissa Paste 92
Mediterranean Herb Blend 93
Mint Yogurt Sauce 93
Red Wine Vinaigrette 94
Chimichurri Sauce 94
Artichoke and Olive Tapenade 95
Sun-Dried Tomato and Basil Spread 95

CHAPTER 13. DESERT 96

Greek Yogurt with Honey and Walnuts ... 96
Orange Blossom Semolina Cake 96
Date and Walnut Bars 97
Honey Almond Biscotti 97
Almond and Apricot Cake 98
Orange Cardamom Cookies 98
Poached Pears with Red Wine 99
Pistachio Baklava Rolls 99
Honey and Cinnamon Roasted Figs 100
Spiced Apple and Walnut Cake 100

Fig and Ricotta Tartlets 101
Lemon and Almond Tart 101
Honey and Nut Stuffed Dates 102
Orange and Olive Oil Muffins 102

APPENDIX MEASUREMENT CONVERSION CHART 103

APPENDIX 30-DAY MEAL PLAN 104

APPENDIX RECIPES INDEX 105

INTRODUCTION

Welcome to "The Simple Mediterranean Diet Cookbook for Beginners," your gateway to a culinary journey that will transport you to the sun-drenched shores of the Mediterranean. This isn't just a cookbook; it's a celebration of a way of life that has delighted taste buds and nourished bodies for centuries.

Imagine the vibrant flavors of ripe olives, juicy tomatoes, and fragrant herbs mingling together to create dishes that are as delightful to eat as they are to prepare. This book is your passport to the heart-healthy, mouth-watering world of the Mediterranean diet—a lifestyle that celebrates each meal as an occasion and the kitchen as a canvas for your culinary artistry.

Within these pages, you'll discover the secrets to longevity, health, and happiness, all inspired by the diverse cultures and rich culinary traditions of the Mediterranean region. From the aromatic spices of Morocco to the fresh, simple delights of Greek salads, each recipe is crafted to bring the Mediterranean magic to your kitchen.

So, whether you're a seasoned home cook or a complete beginner, grab your apron and olive oil, and get ready to embark on a journey where every meal is more than just sustenance—it's a celebration of life, love, and togetherness. This cookbook will guide you through easy-to-follow recipes, bursting with flavor and nutrition, ensuring that you can enjoy the benefits of the Mediterranean diet effortlessly.

Get ready to indulge in the goodness of the Mediterranean, one delicious recipe at a time. Let the cooking adventures begin, and may your kitchen be filled with the warmth, joy, and magic of Mediterranean cuisine!

CHAPTER 1. LIFESTYLE ADVICE

MASTERING THE SIMPLE MEDITERRANEAN DIET FOR BEGINNERS: TECHNIQUES, TIPS, AND TRICKS

The Simple Mediterranean Diet Cookbook for Beginners offers an accessible and delicious way to embrace healthier eating habits. This comprehensive guide will help you maximize your success and enjoyment while adhering to the diet's principles. We'll cover meal planning, grocery shopping, cooking methods, dining out, and overcoming common obstacles.

MEAL PLANNING

Weekly Menu Strategies
1. **Balance Nutrients:** Ensure each meal includes a variety of nutrients. Aim for a balance of proteins, healthy fats, and carbohydrates. Include vegetables, fruits, whole grains, legumes, nuts, and seeds.
2. **Diverse Food Choices:** Rotate different types of proteins (fish, poultry, legumes) and vegetables to keep meals interesting. This variety ensures you get a wide range of vitamins and minerals.
3. **Prep in Advance:** Prepare ingredients in advance, such as chopping vegetables, cooking grains, and marinating proteins. This saves time and makes cooking easier.
4. **Use a Template:** Create a basic template for your meals. For example, designate Mondays for fish, Tuesdays for vegetarian dishes, Wednesdays for poultry, and so on.

GROCERY SHOPPING

Efficient Shopping Tips
1. **Read Labels:** Look for products with minimal ingredients and avoid processed foods. Check for added sugars and unhealthy fats.
2. **Fresh and Nutritious Options:** Choose fresh, whole foods. Opt for organic when possible, and prioritize seasonal produce for better taste and nutrition.
3. **Cost-Saving Tips:** Buy in bulk to save money on nuts, seeds, grains, and legumes. Purchase seasonal produce and consider joining a local CSA (Community Supported Agriculture) for fresh, local vegetables.

Shopping List Essentials
- **Fruits and Vegetables:** Tomatoes, cucumbers, leafy greens, berries, apples, and citrus fruits.
- **Proteins:** Fish (especially fatty fish like salmon), chicken, beans, and lentils.
- **Healthy Fats:** Olive oil, avocados, nuts, and seeds.
- **Whole Grains:** Brown rice, quinoa, whole wheat pasta, and barley.
- **Dairy:** Greek yogurt, feta cheese, and other minimally processed cheeses.

COOKING METHODS

Enhancing Flavor and Nutrition
1. **Grilling and Roasting:** These methods bring out natural flavors without adding extra fats. Perfect for vegetables, fish, and lean meats.
2. **Sautéing and Stir-Frying:** Use olive oil to sauté or stir-fry vegetables and proteins. These techniques are quick and preserve nutrients.
3. **Steaming and Poaching:** These gentle cooking methods help maintain the texture and nutrients of vegetables and fish.
4. **Herbs and Spices:** Enhance flavor with herbs like basil, oregano, and thyme, and spices like cumin, paprika, and turmeric. They add complexity without extra calories.

DINING OUT

Sticking to the Diet
1. **Research Ahead:** Look up restaurant menus online and choose places with Mediterranean-friendly options.
2. **Communicate Dietary Needs:** Don't hesitate to ask servers about ingredient preparations. Request modifications to suit your diet.

3. **Smart Choices:** Opt for grilled or roasted dishes, salads with olive oil dressing, and avoid fried or heavily sauced foods.
4. **Portion Control:** Mediterranean diet emphasizes moderate portions. Share dishes or ask for a half portion if available.

OVERCOMING CHALLENGES

Social Events and Cravings
1. **Bring a Dish:** If attending a potluck or party, bring a Mediterranean-friendly dish to ensure you have a healthy option.
2. **Snack Wisely:** Keep healthy snacks like nuts, fruits, and hummus on hand to combat cravings.
3. **Mindful Eating:** Focus on enjoying your food and eating slowly to recognize when you're full.

Handling Slip-Ups
1. **Stay Positive:** Don't dwell on dietary slip-ups. Recognize them as temporary and get back on track with your next meal.

2. **Plan for Success:** Identify potential challenges ahead of time and plan strategies to handle them.
3. **Support System:** Engage with a community or find a diet buddy for mutual support and motivation.

CONCLUSION

Adopting the Simple Mediterranean Diet for Beginners is a rewarding journey toward better health. By incorporating these practical tips for meal planning, grocery shopping, cooking, and dining out, you can enhance your success and enjoyment on the diet. Remember, the key is consistency, variety, and enjoying the rich flavors and health benefits that come with this time-honored way of eating. Happy cooking and bon appétit!

CHAPTER 2. BREAKFAST

Avocado Toast with Cherry Tomatoes

Prep Time: **10 mins** | Cook Time: **5 mins**
Yield: **2 servings**

INGREDIENTS:

- 2 slices whole-grain bread
- 1 ripe avocado
- 1 cup cherry tomatoes, halved
- 1 tbsp olive oil
- Salt & pepper to taste
- **Optional:**
  - 1 tsp lemon juice
  - 1/4 tsp red pepper flakes
  - Fresh basil or parsley, chopped

INSTRUCTIONS:

1. **Toast Bread:**
   - Toast bread slices to desired crispness.
2. **Prepare Avocado:**
   - Mash avocado in a bowl; mix in salt, pepper, and lemon juice.
3. **Sauté Tomatoes:**
   - Heat olive oil in a skillet over medium heat. Sauté cherry tomatoes for 2-3 minutes until slightly soft.
4. **Assemble:**
   - Spread mashed avocado on toasted bread. Top with sautéed cherry tomatoes.
5. **Garnish:**
   - Sprinkle with red pepper flakes and fresh herbs if desired. Serve immediately.

NUTRITION (PER SERVING):

- **Calories:** 250
- **Protein:** 5g
- **Carbs:** 28g
- **Fats:** 15g
- **Fiber:** 8g
- **Sodium:** 150mg

Shakshuka (Poached Eggs in Tomato Sauce)

Prep Time: **10 mins** | Cook Time: **20 mins**
Yield: **4 servings**

INGREDIENTS:

- 4 large eggs
- 2 tbsp olive oil
- 1 onion, diced
- 1 red bell pepper, diced
- 2 cloves garlic, minced
- 1 can (14 oz) diced tomatoes
- 1 tsp ground cumin
- 1 tsp paprika
- Salt & pepper to taste
- **Optional:**
  - 1/4 tsp cayenne pepper
  - Fresh parsley, chopped

INSTRUCTIONS:

1. **Sauté Vegetables:**
   - Heat olive oil in a skillet over medium heat. Sauté onion, bell pepper, and garlic until soft.
2. **Add Spices:**
   - Stir in cumin, paprika, salt, pepper, and cayenne if using. Cook for 1 minute.
3. **Simmer Sauce:**
   - Add diced tomatoes. Simmer for 10 minutes until sauce thickens.
4. **Poach Eggs:**
   - Make 4 wells in the sauce. Crack an egg into each well. Cover and cook until eggs are set (5-8 minutes).
5. **Garnish:**
   - Sprinkle with fresh parsley. Serve hot.

NUTRITION (PER SERVING):

- **Calories:** 180
- **Protein:** 8g
- **Carbs:** 12g
- **Fats:** 12g
- **Fiber:** 3g
- **Sodium:** 350mg

Mediterranean Breakfast Bowl

Prep Time: **20 mins** | Cook Time: **10 mins**
Yield: **4 servings**

INGREDIENTS:

- **Base:** 1 cup cooked quinoa or farro
- **Protein:** 4 large eggs
- **Veggies:**
  - 1 cup cherry tomatoes, halved
  - 1 cucumber, diced
  - 1 red bell pepper, diced
  - 1/4 cup red onion, sliced
  - 1 cup baby spinach
- **Toppings:**
  - 1/4 cup kalamata olives, sliced
  - 1/4 cup feta cheese, crumbled
  - 2 tbsp fresh parsley, chopped
- **Dressing:**
  - 1/4 cup olive oil
  - 2 tbsp lemon juice
  - 1 garlic clove, minced
  - Salt & pepper
- **Optional:**
  - 1 tsp oregano
  - 1 tsp smoked paprika

INSTRUCTIONS:

1. **Cook Grains:** Prepare quinoa or farro as per package.
2. **Prep Veggies:** Halve tomatoes, dice cucumber and pepper, slice onion.
3. **Cook Eggs:** Fry, scramble, or poach eggs in a skillet; season with salt and pepper.
4. **Make Dressing:** Mix olive oil, lemon juice, garlic, salt, pepper, oregano, and paprika.
5. **Assemble:** Divide grains, veggies, and eggs in bowls. Add olives, feta, parsley.
6. **Drizzle Dressing:** Evenly distribute dressing over bowls. Serve immediately.

NUTRITION (PER SERVING):

- **Calories:** 320
- **Protein:** 14g
- **Carbs:** 22g
- **Fats:** 21g
- **Fiber:** 5g
- **Sodium:** 450mg

Spinach and Feta Frittata

Prep Time: **10 mins** | Cook Time: **20 mins**
Yield: **4 servings**

INGREDIENTS:

- 6 large eggs
- 1/4 cup milk
- 1 cup fresh spinach, chopped
- 1/2 cup feta cheese, crumbled
- 1 small onion, diced
- 1 clove garlic, minced
- 1 tbsp olive oil
- Salt & pepper to taste
- **Optional:**
  - 1 tsp dried oregano
  - 1 tsp dried dill

INSTRUCTIONS:

1. **Preheat Oven:**
   - Preheat oven to 375°F (190°C).
2. **Sauté Vegetables:**
   - Heat olive oil in an oven-safe skillet over medium heat. Sauté onion and garlic until soft. Add spinach; cook until wilted.
3. **Prepare Egg Mixture:**
   - In a bowl, whisk eggs, milk, salt, pepper, oregano, and dill.
4. **Combine:**
   - Pour egg mixture over sautéed vegetables in the skillet. Sprinkle feta cheese on top.
5. **Cook:**
   - Cook on stovetop for 2-3 minutes until edges set.
6. **Bake:**
   - Transfer skillet to oven. Bake for 15-20 minutes until the frittata is set and golden.
7. **Serve:**
   - Slice and serve warm.

NUTRITION (PER SERVING):

- **Calories:** 200
- **Protein:** 12g
- **Carbs:** 5g
- **Fats:** 15g
- **Fiber:** 1g
- **Sodium:** 350mg

Quinoa Breakfast Porridge

Prep Time: **5 mins** | Cook Time: **20 mins**
Yield: **4 servings**

INGREDIENTS:

- 1 cup quinoa, rinsed
- 2 cups almond milk (or any milk)
- 1 cup water
- 1 tsp vanilla extract
- 1 tbsp honey or maple syrup
- **Optional Toppings:**
  - Fresh berries
  - Sliced banana
  - Chopped nuts
  - Cinnamon

INSTRUCTIONS:

1. **Cook Quinoa:**
   - Combine quinoa, almond milk, and water in a pot. Bring to a boil.
2. **Simmer:**
   - Reduce heat and simmer for 15 minutes until quinoa is tender.
3. **Flavor:**
   - Stir in vanilla extract and honey. Cook for an additional 5 minutes.
4. **Serve:**
   - Divide into bowls and add desired toppings.

NUTRITION (PER SERVING):

- **Calories:** 180
- **Protein:** 6g
- **Carbs:** 32g
- **Fats:** 3g
- **Fiber:** 3g
- **Sodium:** 30mg

Enjoy your healthy and flavorful Quinoa Breakfast Porridge!

Mediterranean Omelette with Sun-Dried Tomatoes

Prep Time: **5 mins** | Cook Time: **10 mins**
Yield: **2 servings**

INGREDIENTS:

- 4 large eggs
- 1/4 cup milk
- 1/4 cup sun-dried tomatoes, chopped
- 1/4 cup feta cheese, crumbled
- 1/2 cup spinach, chopped
- 1 tbsp olive oil
- Salt & pepper to taste
- **Optional:**
  - 1 tsp dried oregano
  - Fresh basil, chopped

INSTRUCTIONS:

1. **Whisk Eggs:**
   - Beat eggs with milk, salt, pepper, and oregano.
2. **Sauté Spinach:**
   - Heat olive oil in a skillet over medium heat. Sauté spinach until wilted.
3. **Cook Omelette:**
   - Pour egg mixture into skillet. Cook until edges start to set.
4. **Add Fillings:**
   - Sprinkle sun-dried tomatoes and feta cheese over eggs. Cook until set.
5. **Fold & Serve:**
   - Fold omelette in half, garnish with basil. Serve hot.

NUTRITION (PER SERVING):

- **Calories:** 220
- **Protein:** 14g
- **Carbs:** 6g
- **Fats:** 16g
- **Fiber:** 2g
- **Sodium:** 400mg

Enjoy your healthy and flavorful Mediterranean Omelette with Sun-Dried Tomatoes!

Hummus Toast with Cucumbers and Radishes

Prep Time: **5 mins** | Cook Time: **0 mins**
Yield: **2 servings**

INGREDIENTS:

- 2 slices whole-grain bread
- 1/2 cup hummus
- 1/2 cucumber, thinly sliced
- 4 radishes, thinly sliced
- **Optional:**
  - 1 tbsp fresh dill or parsley, chopped
  - 1/4 tsp red pepper flakes
  - Lemon zest

INSTRUCTIONS:

1. **Toast Bread:**
   - Toast bread slices to desired crispness.
2. **Spread Hummus:**
   - Spread hummus evenly on each slice.
3. **Add Toppings:**
   - Top with cucumber and radish slices.
4. **Garnish:**
   - Sprinkle with dill, red pepper flakes, and lemon zest if desired. Serve immediately.

NUTRITION (PER SERVING):

- **Calories:** 200
- **Protein:** 6g
- **Carbs:** 28g
- **Fats:** 8g
- **Fiber:** 6g
- **Sodium:** 350mg

Enjoy your healthy and flavorful Hummus Toast with Cucumbers and Radishes!

Whole Wheat Pancakes with Fresh Berries

Prep Time: **10 mins** | Cook Time: **15 mins**
Yield: **4 servings**

INGREDIENTS:

- 1 cup whole wheat flour
- 1 tbsp baking powder
- 1/2 tsp salt
- 1 cup milk
- 1 large egg
- 1 tbsp honey or maple syrup
- 1 tsp vanilla extract
- 1 tbsp olive oil
- **Toppings:** Fresh berries, honey, or yogurt

INSTRUCTIONS:

1. **Mix Dry Ingredients:**
   - Combine flour, baking powder, and salt in a bowl.
2. **Mix Wet Ingredients:**
   - In another bowl, whisk milk, egg, honey, vanilla, and olive oil.
3. **Combine:**
   - Pour wet ingredients into dry ingredients; mix until just combined.
4. **Cook Pancakes:**
   - Heat a skillet over medium heat. Pour batter onto skillet, cook until bubbles form, then flip and cook until golden.
5. **Serve:**
   - Top with fresh berries and your choice of honey or yogurt.

NUTRITION (PER SERVING):

- **Calories:** 250
- **Protein:** 7g
- **Carbs:** 40g
- **Fats:** 8g
- **Fiber:** 5g
- **Sodium:** 300mg

Enjoy your healthy and flavorful Whole Wheat Pancakes with Fresh Berries!

Mediterranean Breakfast Tacos

Prep Time: **10 mins** | Cook Time: **10 mins**
Yield: **4 servings**

INGREDIENTS:

- 4 whole-grain tortillas
- 4 large eggs
- 1/2 cup cherry tomatoes, halved
- 1/2 cup cucumber, diced
- 1/4 cup feta cheese, crumbled
- 1/4 cup red onion, diced
- 1 tbsp olive oil
- Salt & pepper to taste
- **Optional:**
  - 1 tbsp fresh parsley, chopped
  - 1/4 tsp paprika

INSTRUCTIONS:

1. **Cook Eggs:**
   - Scramble eggs in olive oil over medium heat; season with salt and pepper.
2. **Prepare Veggies:**
   - Dice cherry tomatoes, cucumber, and red onion.
3. **Assemble Tacos:**
   - Place scrambled eggs on tortillas, top with veggies, feta, and parsley.
4. **Serve:**
   - Sprinkle with paprika if desired. Serve immediately.

NUTRITION (PER SERVING):

- **Calories:** 250
- **Protein:** 12g
- **Carbs:** 24g
- **Fats:** 12g
- **Fiber:** 4g
- **Sodium:** 350mg

Enjoy your healthy and flavorful Mediterranean Breakfast Tacos!

Mediterranean Smoothie Bowl

Prep Time: **5 mins** | Cook Time: **0 mins**
Yield: **2 servings**

INGREDIENTS:

- 1 cup Greek yogurt
- 1 cup mixed berries (frozen or fresh)
- 1 banana
- 1 tbsp honey
- **Optional Toppings:**
  - Sliced almonds
  - Fresh berries
  - Chia seeds
  - Granola

INSTRUCTIONS:

1. **Blend Base:**
   - Blend Greek yogurt, berries, banana, and honey until smooth.
2. **Serve:**
   - Pour into bowls.
3. **Add Toppings:**
   - Top with sliced almonds, fresh berries, chia seeds, and granola.

NUTRITION (PER SERVING):

- **Calories:** 220
- **Protein:** 10g
- **Carbs:** 36g
- **Fats:** 5g
- **Fiber:** 6g
- **Sodium:** 70mg

Enjoy your healthy and flavorful Mediterranean Smoothie Bowl!

Herbed Goat Cheese and Vegetable Muffins

Prep Time: **10 mins** | Cook Time: **25 mins**
Yield: **12 muffins**

INGREDIENTS:

- 1 cup whole wheat flour
- 1 tsp baking powder
- 1/2 tsp baking soda
- 1/4 tsp salt
- 1/2 cup goat cheese, crumbled
- 1 cup grated zucchini
- 1/2 cup diced red bell pepper
- 1/4 cup chopped fresh herbs (e.g., parsley, dill)
- 2 large eggs
- 1/2 cup milk
- 1/4 cup olive oil

INSTRUCTIONS:

1. **Preheat Oven:**
   - Preheat to 350°F (175°C). Grease muffin tin.
2. **Mix Dry Ingredients:**
   - Combine flour, baking powder, baking soda, and salt.
3. **Mix Wet Ingredients:**
   - In another bowl, whisk eggs, milk, and olive oil.
4. **Combine:**
   - Add wet ingredients to dry. Fold in goat cheese, zucchini, bell pepper, and herbs.
5. **Bake:**
   - Divide batter into muffin tin. Bake for 25 mins or until golden brown.
6. **Cool:**
   - Let cool before serving.

NUTRITION (PER MUFFIN):

- **Calories:** 120
- **Protein:** 4g
- **Carbs:** 12g
- **Fats:** 7g
- **Fiber:** 2g
- **Sodium:** 150mg

Lemon Ricotta Pancakes

Prep Time: **10 mins** | Cook Time: **15 mins**
Yield: **4 servings**

INGREDIENTS:

- 1 cup whole wheat flour
- 1 tbsp baking powder
- 1/4 tsp salt
- 3/4 cup ricotta cheese
- 1 cup milk
- 2 large eggs
- 2 tbsp honey
- 1 tsp vanilla extract
- Zest of 1 lemon
- **Optional Toppings:** Fresh berries, honey, or yogurt

INSTRUCTIONS:

1. **Mix Dry Ingredients:**
   - Combine flour, baking powder, and salt in a bowl.
2. **Mix Wet Ingredients:**
   - In another bowl, whisk ricotta, milk, eggs, honey, vanilla, and lemon zest.
3. **Combine:**
   - Add wet ingredients to dry; mix until just combined.
4. **Cook Pancakes:**
   - Heat a skillet over medium heat. Pour batter onto skillet, cook until bubbles form, flip, and cook until golden.
5. **Serve:**
   - Top with fresh berries, honey, or yogurt.

NUTRITION (PER SERVING):

- **Calories:** 220
- **Protein:** 10g
- **Carbs:** 30g
- **Fats:** 8g
- **Fiber:** 2g
- **Sodium:** 220mg

Egg and Veggie Breakfast Wrap

Prep Time: **5 mins** | Cook Time: **10 mins**
Yield: **2 servings**

INGREDIENTS:

- 2 whole-grain tortillas
- 4 large eggs
- 1/2 cup bell peppers, diced
- 1/2 cup spinach, chopped
- 1/4 cup feta cheese, crumbled
- 1 tbsp olive oil
- Salt & pepper to taste
- **Optional:** Hot sauce, fresh herbs

INSTRUCTIONS:

1. **Whisk Eggs:**
   - Beat eggs with salt and pepper.
2. **Cook Veggies:**
   - Sauté bell peppers and spinach in olive oil over medium heat until soft.
3. **Scramble Eggs:**
   - Pour eggs into skillet, cook until set.
4. **Assemble Wraps:**
   - Divide egg mixture between tortillas, top with feta.
5. **Serve:**
   - Add optional hot sauce or herbs. Roll up and serve warm.

NUTRITION (PER SERVING):

- **Calories:** 300
- **Protein:** 16g
- **Carbs:** 28g
- **Fats:** 14g
- **Fiber:** 4g
- **Sodium:** 400mg

Enjoy your healthy and flavorful Egg and Veggie Breakfast Wrap!

Feta and Spinach Muffins

Prep Time: **10 mins** | Cook Time: **25 mins**
Yield: **12 muffins**

INGREDIENTS:

- 1 cup whole wheat flour
- 1 tsp baking powder
- 1/2 tsp baking soda
- 1/4 tsp salt
- 1/2 cup crumbled feta cheese
- 1 cup fresh spinach, chopped
- 2 large eggs
- 1/2 cup milk
- 1/4 cup olive oil

INSTRUCTIONS:

1. **Preheat Oven:**
   - Preheat to 350°F (175°C). Grease muffin tin.
2. **Mix Dry Ingredients:**
   - Combine flour, baking powder, baking soda, and salt.
3. **Mix Wet Ingredients:**
   - Whisk eggs, milk, and olive oil in another bowl.
4. **Combine:**
   - Add wet ingredients to dry, fold in feta and spinach.
5. **Bake:**
   - Divide batter into muffin tin. Bake for 25 mins or until golden brown.
6. **Cool:**
   - Let cool before serving.

NUTRITION (PER MUFFIN):

- **Calories:** 120
- **Protein:** 4g
- **Carbs:** 12g
- **Fats:** 7g
- **Fiber:** 2g
- **Sodium:** 150mg

Millet Porridge with Nuts and Fruits

Prep Time: **5 mins** | Cook Time: **20 mins**
Yield: **2 servings**

INGREDIENTS:

- 1 cup millet
- 2 cups water
- 1/2 cup milk
- 2 tbsp honey
- 1/4 cup mixed nuts, chopped
- **Optional Toppings:** Fresh fruits, cinnamon

INSTRUCTIONS:

1. **Cook Millet:**
   - Rinse millet. Combine with water in a pot, bring to a boil. Reduce heat, simmer for 15 mins.
2. **Add Milk and Honey:**
   - Stir in milk and honey, cook for 5 mins until creamy.
3. **Add Toppings:**
   - Top with nuts and optional fruits or cinnamon.
4. **Serve:**
   - Enjoy warm.

NUTRITION (PER SERVING):

- **Calories:** 300
- **Protein:** 8g
- **Carbs:** 50g
- **Fats:** 10g
- **Fiber:** 6g
- **Sodium:** 30mg

Enjoy your healthy and flavorful Millet Porridge with Nuts and Fruits!

Tofu Scramble with Mediterranean Veggies

Prep Time: 10 mins | Cook Time: 10 mins
Yield: 2 servings

INGREDIENTS:

- 1 block firm tofu, crumbled
- 1 tbsp olive oil
- 1/2 cup cherry tomatoes, halved
- 1/2 cup bell pepper, diced
- 1/4 cup red onion, diced
- 1 cup spinach, chopped
- 1 tsp turmeric
- Salt & pepper to taste
- **Optional:** Fresh basil or parsley, chopped

INSTRUCTIONS:

1. **Sauté Veggies:**
   - Heat olive oil in a skillet over medium heat. Sauté tomatoes, bell pepper, and onion until soft.
2. **Add Tofu:**
   - Stir in crumbled tofu and turmeric, cook for 5 mins.
3. **Add Spinach:**
   - Add spinach, cook until wilted. Season with salt and pepper.
4. **Garnish:**
   - Top with fresh basil or parsley if desired. Serve warm.

NUTRITION (PER SERVING):

- **Calories:** 250
- **Protein:** 18g
- **Carbs:** 10g
- **Fats:** 15g
- **Fiber:** 4g
- **Sodium:** 300mg

Enjoy your healthy and flavorful Tofu Scramble with Mediterranean Veggies!

CHAPTER 3. SALADS

Mediterranean Chickpea Salad

Prep Time: **10 mins** | Cooking Time: **None**
Yield: **4 portions**

INGREDIENTS:

- 2 cups chickpeas, cooked or canned
- 1 cup cherry tomatoes, halved
- 1 cucumber, diced
- 1/4 cup red onion, finely chopped
- 1/4 cup Kalamata olives, halved
- 1/4 cup feta cheese, crumbled
- 1/4 cup parsley, chopped
- 2 tbsp olive oil
- 2 tbsp lemon juice
- Salt and pepper to taste

INSTRUCTIONS:

1. **Combine Ingredients:**
   Mix chickpeas, tomatoes, cucumber, onion, olives, feta, and parsley in a bowl.
2. **Make Dressing:**
   Whisk olive oil, lemon juice, salt, and pepper.
3. **Assemble:**
   Pour dressing over salad and toss.
4. **Serve:**
   Serve immediately or chill.

NUTRITIONAL INFORMATION (PER SERVING):

- **Calories:** 200
- **Protein:** 7g
- **Carbohydrates:** 24g
- **Fat:** 8g
- **Fiber:** 6g
- **Sodium:** 350mg

Enjoy your healthy and flavorful Chickpea Salad!

Spinach Salad with Pomegranate and Walnuts

Prep Time: **10 mins** | Cooking Time: **None**
Yield: **4 portions**

INGREDIENTS:

- 4 cups spinach, fresh
- 1 cup pomegranate seeds
- 1/2 cup walnuts, chopped
- 1/4 cup feta cheese, crumbled
- 2 tbsp olive oil
- 2 tbsp balsamic vinegar
- Salt and pepper to taste

INSTRUCTIONS:

1. **Combine Ingredients:**
   Mix spinach, pomegranate seeds, walnuts, and feta in a bowl.
2. **Make Dressing:**
   Whisk olive oil, balsamic vinegar, salt, and pepper.
3. **Assemble:**
   Pour dressing over salad and toss.
4. **Serve:**
   Serve immediately.

NUTRITIONAL INFORMATION (PER SERVING):

- **Calories:** 220
- **Protein:** 5g
- **Carbohydrates:** 15g
- **Fat:** 18g
- **Fiber:** 4g
- **Sodium:** 180mg

Enjoy your healthy and flavorful Spinach Salad!

Tabbouleh with Fresh Herbs and Lemon

Prep Time: **20 mins** | Cooking Time: **None**
Yield: **4 portions**

INGREDIENTS:

- 1 cup bulgur wheat
- 2 cups boiling water
- 1 cup fresh parsley, finely chopped
- 1/2 cup fresh mint, finely chopped
- 2 cups tomatoes, diced
- 1 cucumber, diced
- 1/4 cup red onion, finely chopped
- 1/4 cup extra-virgin olive oil
- 1/4 cup fresh lemon juice
- Salt and pepper to taste

INSTRUCTIONS:

1. **Prepare Bulgur:**
   - Place bulgur in a bowl, pour boiling water over it, cover, and let sit for 15 minutes. Drain any excess water.
2. **Combine Ingredients:**
   - In a large bowl, mix soaked bulgur, parsley, mint, tomatoes, cucumber, and red onion.
3. **Make Dressing:**
   - Whisk olive oil, lemon juice, salt, and pepper in a small bowl.
4. **Assemble:**
   - Pour dressing over the salad, toss to coat.
5. **Serve:**
   - Serve immediately or chill for up to an hour for enhanced flavor.

NUTRITIONAL INFORMATION (PER SERVING):

- **Calories:** 180
- **Protein:** 4g
- **Carbohydrates:** 25g
- **Fat:** 8g
- **Fiber:** 6g
- **Sodium:** 150mg

Enjoy your fresh and healthy Tabbouleh!

Greek Salad with Feta and Olives

Prep Time: **15 mins** | Cooking Time: **None**
Yield: **4 portions**

INGREDIENTS:

- **Salad:**
  - 4 cups Romaine lettuce, chopped
  - 2 cups cherry tomatoes, halved
  - 1 cucumber, sliced
  - 1 red onion, thinly sliced
  - 1 green bell pepper, sliced
  - 1 cup Kalamata olives, pitted
  - 8 oz feta cheese, cubed or crumbled
- **Dressing:**
  - 1/4 cup extra-virgin olive oil
  - 2 tbsp red wine vinegar
  - 1 tsp dried oregano (optional: fresh herbs like parsley or dill)
  - 1 clove garlic, minced
  - Salt and pepper to taste

INSTRUCTIONS:

1. **Prepare Salad:**
   - Combine Romaine lettuce, cherry tomatoes, cucumber, red onion, green bell pepper, and Kalamata olives in a large bowl.
2. **Make Dressing:**
   - Whisk olive oil, red wine vinegar, dried oregano, minced garlic, salt, and pepper in a small bowl.
3. **Assemble:**
   - Drizzle dressing over salad, toss to coat, and top with feta cheese.
4. **Serve:**
   - Serve immediately or chill for up to an hour for enhanced flavor.

NUTRITIONAL INFORMATION (PER SERVING):

- **Calories:** 290
- **Protein:** 8g
- **Carbohydrates:** 12g
- **Fat:** 24g
- **Fiber:** 4g
- **Sodium:** 620mg

Enjoy your Mediterranean-inspired Greek salad!

Warm Farro Salad with Roasted Vegetables

Prep Time: **10 mins** | Cooking Time: **30 mins**
Yield: **4 portions**

INGREDIENTS:

- 1 cup farro
- 3 cups water
- 1 cup cherry tomatoes, halved
- 1 zucchini, diced
- 1 bell pepper, diced
- 1/4 cup red onion, chopped
- 2 tbsp olive oil
- 2 tbsp balsamic vinegar
- Salt and pepper to taste
- **Optional:** fresh herbs (parsley, basil)

INSTRUCTIONS:

1. **Cook Farro:**
   - Boil farro in water for 25 minutes. Drain and set aside.
2. **Roast Vegetables:**
   - Toss tomatoes, zucchini, bell pepper, and onion with 1 tbsp olive oil, salt, and pepper. Roast at 400°F for 20 minutes.
3. **Combine Ingredients:**
   - Mix cooked farro and roasted vegetables in a bowl.
4. **Make Dressing:**
   - Whisk remaining olive oil and balsamic vinegar.
5. **Assemble:**
   - Pour dressing over salad and toss.
6. **Serve:**
   - Serve warm.

NUTRITIONAL INFORMATION (PER SERVING):

- **Calories:** 250
- **Protein:** 7g
- **Carbohydrates:** 40g
- **Fat:** 8g
- **Fiber:** 8g
- **Sodium:** 200mg

Enjoy your healthy and flavorful Warm Farro Salad!

Beet and Orange Salad with Goat Cheese

Prep Time: **10 mins** | Cooking Time: **20 mins**
Yield: **4 portions**

INGREDIENTS:

- 4 beets, roasted and sliced
- 2 oranges, segmented
- 1/4 cup goat cheese, crumbled
- 1/4 cup walnuts, chopped
- 2 tbsp olive oil
- 1 tbsp balsamic vinegar
- Salt and pepper to taste
- **Optional:** fresh mint or parsley

INSTRUCTIONS:

1. **Roast Beets:**
   - Roast beets at 400°F for 20 minutes. Cool and slice.
2. **Combine Ingredients:**
   - Mix beets, oranges, goat cheese, and walnuts in a bowl.
3. **Make Dressing:**
   - Whisk olive oil, balsamic vinegar, salt, and pepper.
4. **Assemble:**
   - Pour dressing over salad and toss.
5. **Serve:**
   - Serve immediately.

NUTRITIONAL INFORMATION (PER SERVING):

- **Calories:** 220
- **Protein:** 5g
- **Carbohydrates:** 24g
- **Fat:** 12g
- **Fiber:** 6g
- **Sodium:** 180mg

Enjoy your healthy and flavorful Beet and Orange Salad!

Roasted Red Pepper and Chickpea Salad

Prep Time: **10 mins** | Cooking Time: **20 mins**
Yield: **4 portions**

INGREDIENTS:

- 2 red bell peppers, roasted and sliced
- 1 can chickpeas, drained
- 1/4 cup red onion, chopped
- 1/4 cup parsley, chopped
- 2 tbsp olive oil
- 1 tbsp lemon juice
- Salt and pepper to taste
- **Optional:** cumin or paprika

INSTRUCTIONS:

1. **Roast Peppers:**
   - Roast bell peppers at 400°F for 20 minutes. Cool and slice.
2. **Combine Ingredients:**
   - Mix roasted peppers, chickpeas, red onion, and parsley in a bowl.
3. **Make Dressing:**
   - Whisk olive oil, lemon juice, salt, pepper, and optional spices.
4. **Assemble:**
   - Pour dressing over salad and toss.
5. **Serve:**
   - Serve immediately.

NUTRITIONAL INFORMATION (PER SERVING):

- **Calories:** 180
- **Protein:** 6g
- **Carbohydrates:** 22g
- **Fat:** 8g
- **Fiber:** 6g
- **Sodium:** 220mg

Enjoy your healthy and flavorful Roasted Red Pepper and Chickpea Salad!

Avocado and Shrimp Salad

Prep Time: **10 mins** | Cooking Time: **5 mins**
Yield: **4 portions**

INGREDIENTS:

- 1 lb shrimp, cooked
- 2 avocados, diced
- 1 cup cherry tomatoes, halved
- 1/4 cup red onion, chopped
- 2 tbsp olive oil
- 1 tbsp lemon juice
- Salt and pepper to taste
- **Optional:** fresh cilantro or parsley

INSTRUCTIONS:

1. **Cook Shrimp:**
   - Sauté shrimp in a skillet for 5 minutes until pink.
2. **Combine Ingredients:**
   - Mix shrimp, avocados, tomatoes, and red onion in a bowl.
3. **Make Dressing:**
   - Whisk olive oil, lemon juice, salt, and pepper.
4. **Assemble:**
   - Pour dressing over salad and toss.
5. **Serve:**
   - Serve immediately.

NUTRITIONAL INFORMATION (PER SERVING):

- **Calories:** 250
- **Protein:** 18g
- **Carbohydrates:** 12g
- **Fat:** 15g
- **Fiber:** 6g
- **Sodium:** 300mg

Enjoy your healthy and flavorful Avocado and Shrimp Salad!

Kale Salad with Lemon and Garlic

Prep Time: **10 mins** | Cooking Time: **None**
Yield: **4 portions**

INGREDIENTS:

- 4 cups kale, chopped
- 1/4 cup lemon juice
- 2 tbsp olive oil
- 2 cloves garlic, minced
- Salt and pepper to taste
- **Optional:** grated Parmesan, red pepper flakes

INSTRUCTIONS:

1. **Prepare Kale:**
   - Massage kale with lemon juice and olive oil until softened.
2. **Add Garlic:**
   - Mix in minced garlic, salt, and pepper.
3. **Customize:**
   - Add Parmesan or red pepper flakes if desired.
4. **Serve:**
   - Serve immediately.

NUTRITIONAL INFORMATION (PER SERVING):

- **Calories:** 100
- **Protein:** 2g
- **Carbohydrates:** 8g
- **Fat:** 7g
- **Fiber:** 2g
- **Sodium:** 150mg

Enjoy your healthy and flavorful Kale Salad!

Tomato and Mozzarella Salad with Basil

Prep Time: **10 mins** | Cooking Time: **None**
Yield: **4 portions**

INGREDIENTS:

- 4 tomatoes, sliced
- 8 oz mozzarella, sliced
- 1/4 cup fresh basil leaves
- 2 tbsp olive oil
- 1 tbsp balsamic vinegar
- Salt and pepper to taste

INSTRUCTIONS:

1. **Arrange Ingredients:**
   - Layer tomatoes and mozzarella on a plate.
2. **Add Basil:**
   - Scatter basil leaves over the top.
3. **Make Dressing:**
   - Drizzle olive oil and balsamic vinegar. Season with salt and pepper.
4. **Serve:**
   - Serve immediately.

NUTRITIONAL INFORMATION (PER SERVING):

- **Calories:** 200
- **Protein:** 10g
- **Carbohydrates:** 6g
- **Fat:** 15g
- **Fiber:** 1g
- **Sodium:** 250mg

Enjoy your healthy and flavorful Tomato and Mozzarella Salad!

Zucchini Noodle Salad with Pesto

Prep Time: **10 mins** | Cooking Time: **None**
Yield: **4 portions**

INGREDIENTS:

- 4 zucchinis, spiralized
- 1/2 cup cherry tomatoes, halved
- 1/4 cup pesto
- Salt and pepper to taste
- **Optional:** grated Parmesan, pine nuts

INSTRUCTIONS:

1. **Prepare Noodles:**
    - Spiralize zucchinis into noodles.
2. **Combine Ingredients:**
    - Mix zucchini noodles, tomatoes, and pesto in a bowl.
3. **Season:**
    - Add salt and pepper. Optional: sprinkle with Parmesan or pine nuts.
4. **Serve:**
    - Serve immediately.

NUTRITIONAL INFORMATION (PER SERVING):

- **Calories:** 120
- **Protein:** 3g
- **Carbohydrates:** 8g
- **Fat:** 9g
- **Fiber:** 2g
- **Sodium:** 180mg

Enjoy your healthy and flavorful Zucchini Noodle Salad!

White Bean and Tuna Salad

Prep Time: **10 mins** | Cooking Time: **None**
Yield: **4 portions**

INGREDIENTS:

- 2 cans white beans, drained
- 2 cans tuna, drained
- 1/2 cup red onion, chopped
- 1/4 cup parsley, chopped
- 2 tbsp olive oil
- 2 tbsp lemon juice
- Salt and pepper to taste

INSTRUCTIONS:

1. **Combine Ingredients:**
    - Mix beans, tuna, onion, and parsley in a bowl.
2. **Make Dressing:**
    - Whisk olive oil, lemon juice, salt, and pepper.
3. **Assemble:**
    - Pour dressing over salad and toss.
4. **Serve:**
    - Serve immediately.

NUTRITIONAL INFORMATION (PER SERVING):

- **Calories:** 250
- **Protein:** 22g
- **Carbohydrates:** 20g
- **Fat:** 8g
- **Fiber:** 6g
- **Sodium:** 300mg

Enjoy your healthy and flavorful White Bean and Tuna Salad!

Caprese Salad with Balsamic Reduction

Prep Time: **10 mins** | Cooking Time: **10 mins**
Yield: **4 portions**

INGREDIENTS:

- 4 tomatoes, sliced
- 8 oz mozzarella, sliced
- 1/4 cup fresh basil leaves
- 1/2 cup balsamic vinegar
- 2 tbsp olive oil
- Salt and pepper to taste

INSTRUCTIONS:

1. **Make Balsamic Reduction:**
   - Simmer balsamic vinegar over low heat until reduced by half.
2. **Arrange Salad:**
   - Layer tomatoes, mozzarella, and basil on a plate.
3. **Add Dressing:**
   - Drizzle with olive oil and balsamic reduction. Season with salt and pepper.
4. **Serve:**
   - Serve immediately.

NUTRITIONAL INFORMATION (PER SERVING):

- **Calories:** 180
- **Protein:** 8g
- **Carbohydrates:** 10g
- **Fat:** 12g
- **Fiber:** 1g
- **Sodium:** 250mg

Enjoy your healthy and flavorful Caprese Salad!

Quinoa and Black Bean Salad

Prep Time: **10 mins** | Cooking Time: **15 mins**
Yield: **4 portions**

INGREDIENTS:

- 1 cup quinoa
- 2 cups water
- 1 can black beans, drained
- 1 cup corn kernels
- 1/2 cup red bell pepper, chopped
- 1/4 cup red onion, chopped
- 1/4 cup cilantro, chopped
- 2 tbsp olive oil
- 2 tbsp lime juice
- Salt and pepper to taste

INSTRUCTIONS:

1. **Cook Quinoa:**
   - Boil quinoa in water for 15 minutes. Cool.
2. **Combine Ingredients:**
   - Mix quinoa, beans, corn, bell pepper, onion, and cilantro in a bowl.
3. **Make Dressing:**
   - Whisk olive oil, lime juice, salt, and pepper.
4. **Assemble:**
   - Pour dressing over salad and toss.
5. **Serve:**
   - Serve immediately.

NUTRITIONAL INFORMATION (PER SERVING):

- **Calories:** 250
- **Protein:** 8g
- **Carbohydrates:** 40g
- **Fat:** 8g
- **Fiber:** 10g
- **Sodium:** 300mg

Enjoy your healthy and flavorful Quinoa and Black Bean Salad!

Roasted Cauliflower and Chickpea Salad

Prep Time: **10 mins** | Cooking Time: **25 mins**
Yield: **4 portions**

INGREDIENTS:

- 1 head cauliflower, chopped
- 1 can chickpeas, drained
- 2 tbsp olive oil
- 1 tsp cumin
- 1 tsp paprika
- Salt and pepper to taste
- 1/4 cup parsley, chopped
- 2 tbsp lemon juice

INSTRUCTIONS:

1. **Roast Vegetables:**
   - Toss cauliflower and chickpeas with olive oil, cumin, paprika, salt, and pepper. Roast at 400°F for 25 minutes.
2. **Combine Ingredients:**
   - Mix roasted cauliflower, chickpeas, and parsley in a bowl.
3. **Add Dressing:**
   - Drizzle with lemon juice and toss.
4. **Serve:**
   - Serve warm.

NUTRITIONAL INFORMATION (PER SERVING):

- **Calories:** 220
- **Protein:** 8g
- **Carbohydrates:** 26g
- **Fat:** 10g
- **Fiber:** 10g
- **Sodium:** 300mg

Enjoy your healthy and flavorful Roasted Cauliflower and Chickpea Salad!

Cucumber and Tomato Salad with Feta

Prep Time: **10 mins** | Cooking Time: **None**
Yield: **4 portions**

INGREDIENTS:

- 2 cucumbers, diced
- 4 tomatoes, diced
- 1/4 cup red onion, chopped
- 1/4 cup feta cheese, crumbled
- 2 tbsp olive oil
- 1 tbsp red wine vinegar
- Salt and pepper to taste
- **Optional:** fresh dill or parsley

INSTRUCTIONS:

1. **Combine Ingredients:**
   - Mix cucumbers, tomatoes, onion, and feta in a bowl.
2. **Make Dressing:**
   - Whisk olive oil, vinegar, salt, and pepper.
3. **Assemble:**
   - Pour dressing over salad and toss. Add dill or parsley if desired.
4. **Serve:**
   - Serve immediately.

NUTRITIONAL INFORMATION (PER SERVING):

- **Calories:** 150
- **Protein:** 4g
- **Carbohydrates:** 12g
- **Fat:** 10g
- **Fiber:** 3g
- **Sodium:** 250mg

Enjoy your healthy and flavorful Cucumber and Tomato Salad with Feta!

Fennel and Orange Salad

Prep Time: **10 mins** | Cooking Time: **None**
Yield: **4 portions**

INGREDIENTS:

- 2 fennel bulbs, thinly sliced
- 2 oranges, segmented
- 1/4 cup red onion, thinly sliced
- 2 tbsp olive oil
- 1 tbsp lemon juice
- Salt and pepper to taste
- **Optional:** fresh mint or parsley

INSTRUCTIONS:

1. **Combine Ingredients:**
   - Mix fennel, oranges, and onion in a bowl.
2. **Make Dressing:**
   - Whisk olive oil, lemon juice, salt, and pepper.
3. **Assemble:**
   - Pour dressing over salad and toss. Add mint or parsley if desired.
4. **Serve:**
   - Serve immediately.

NUTRITIONAL INFORMATION (PER SERVING):

- **Calories:** 120
- **Protein:** 2g
- **Carbohydrates:** 15g
- **Fat:** 7g
- **Fiber:** 4g
- **Sodium:** 50mg

Enjoy your healthy and flavorful Fennel and Orange Salad!

Orzo Salad with Kalamata Olives

Prep Time: **10 mins** | Cooking Time: **10 mins**
Yield: **4 portions**

INGREDIENTS:

- 1 cup orzo
- 1/2 cup Kalamata olives, sliced
- 1 cup cherry tomatoes, halved
- 1/4 cup red onion, chopped
- 1/4 cup feta cheese, crumbled
- 2 tbsp olive oil
- 1 tbsp lemon juice
- Salt and pepper to taste
- **Optional:** fresh parsley or basil

INSTRUCTIONS:

1. **Cook Orzo:**
   - Boil orzo for 10 minutes. Drain and cool.
2. **Combine Ingredients:**
   - Mix orzo, olives, tomatoes, onion, and feta in a bowl.
3. **Make Dressing:**
   - Whisk olive oil, lemon juice, salt, and pepper.
4. **Assemble:**
   - Pour dressing over salad and toss. Add parsley or basil if desired.
5. **Serve:**
   - Serve immediately.

NUTRITIONAL INFORMATION (PER SERVING):

- **Calories:** 250
- **Protein:** 7g
- **Carbohydrates:** 35g
- **Fat:** 10g
- **Fiber:** 3g
- **Sodium:** 300mg

Enjoy your healthy and flavorful Orzo Salad with Kalamata Olives!

CHAPTER 4. MEAT AND POULTRY

Mediterranean Meatballs in Tomato Sauce

Prep Time: **10 mins** | Cooking Time: **20 mins**
Yield: **4 portions**

INGREDIENTS:

- 1 lb ground beef or lamb
- 1/4 cup breadcrumbs
- 1/4 cup parsley, chopped
- 1 egg
- 1 tsp garlic powder
- 1 tsp cumin
- Salt and pepper to taste
- 2 tbsp olive oil
- 2 cups tomato sauce

INSTRUCTIONS:

1. **Make Meatballs:**
   - Mix beef, breadcrumbs, parsley, egg, garlic powder, cumin, salt, and pepper. Form into balls.
2. **Cook Meatballs:**
   - Brown meatballs in olive oil in a skillet over medium heat.
3. **Add Sauce:**
   - Pour tomato sauce over meatballs. Simmer for 15 minutes.
4. **Serve:**
   - Serve immediately.

NUTRITIONAL INFORMATION (PER SERVING):

- **Calories:** 350
- **Protein:** 25g
- **Carbohydrates:** 12g
- **Fat:** 22g
- **Fiber:** 3g
- **Sodium:** 400mg

Enjoy your healthy and flavorful Mediterranean Meatballs in Tomato Sauce!

Braised Lamb with Apricots

Prep Time: **10 mins** | Cooking Time: **1 hour**
Yield: **4 portions**

INGREDIENTS:

- 1 lb lamb shoulder, cubed
- 1 cup dried apricots, halved
- 1 onion, chopped
- 2 cloves garlic, minced
- 1 tsp cinnamon
- 1 tsp cumin
- 1 tbsp olive oil
- 2 cups chicken broth
- Salt and pepper to taste

INSTRUCTIONS:

1. **Brown Lamb:**
   - Sauté lamb in olive oil until browned.
2. **Add Aromatics:**
   - Add onion and garlic, cook until soft.
3. **Combine Ingredients:**
   - Add apricots, cinnamon, cumin, salt, pepper, and broth.
4. **Braise:**
   - Cover and simmer for 1 hour.
5. **Serve:**
   - Serve immediately.

NUTRITIONAL INFORMATION (PER SERVING):

- **Calories:** 400
- **Protein:** 25g
- **Carbohydrates:** 30g
- **Fat:** 20g
- **Fiber:** 5g
- **Sodium:** 350mg

Enjoy your healthy and flavorful Braised Lamb with Apricots!

Chicken Shawarma with Tahini Sauce

Prep Time: **10 mins** | Cooking Time: **20 mins**
Yield: **4 portions**

INGREDIENTS:

- 1 lb chicken thighs, sliced
- 2 tbsp olive oil
- 1 tbsp lemon juice
- 2 tsp cumin
- 2 tsp paprika
- 1 tsp turmeric
- 1 tsp garlic powder
- Salt and pepper to taste

Tahini Sauce:
- 1/4 cup tahini
- 2 tbsp lemon juice
- 2 tbsp water
- 1 clove garlic, minced
- Salt to taste

INSTRUCTIONS:

1. **Marinate Chicken:**
   - Mix chicken with olive oil, lemon juice, cumin, paprika, turmeric, garlic powder, salt, and pepper. Marinate for 10 minutes.
2. **Cook Chicken:**
   - Sauté in a skillet over medium heat for 15-20 minutes until cooked.
3. **Make Tahini Sauce:**
   - Whisk tahini, lemon juice, water, garlic, and salt.
4. **Serve:**
   - Drizzle sauce over chicken and serve immediately.

NUTRITIONAL INFORMATION (PER SERVING):

- **Calories:** 350
- **Protein:** 25g
- **Carbohydrates:** 6g
- **Fat:** 24g
- **Fiber:** 2g
- **Sodium:** 300mg

Enjoy your healthy and flavorful Chicken Shawarma with Tahini Sauce!

Stuffed Peppers with Ground Turkey

Prep Time: **10 mins** | Cooking Time: **30 mins**
Yield: **4 portions**

INGREDIENTS:

- 4 bell peppers, halved and seeded
- 1 lb ground turkey
- 1 cup cooked quinoa
- 1/2 cup diced tomatoes
- 1/4 cup onion, chopped
- 1 tsp garlic powder
- 1 tsp paprika
- 1 tbsp olive oil
- Salt and pepper to taste
- **Optional:** fresh parsley

INSTRUCTIONS:

1. **Cook Turkey:**
   - Sauté turkey and onion in olive oil until browned. Add garlic powder, paprika, salt, and pepper.
2. **Mix Filling:**
   - Combine cooked turkey, quinoa, and tomatoes.
3. **Stuff Peppers:**
   - Fill bell peppers with the mixture.
4. **Bake:**
   - Bake at 375°F for 30 minutes.
5. **Serve:**
   - Garnish with parsley if desired.

NUTRITIONAL INFORMATION (PER SERVING):

- **Calories:** 300
- **Protein:** 28g
- **Carbohydrates:** 20g
- **Fat:** 12g
- **Fiber:** 5g
- **Sodium:** 350mg

Enjoy your healthy and flavorful Stuffed Peppers with Ground Turkey!

Chicken Cacciatore

Prep Time: **10 mins** | Cooking Time: **40 mins**
Yield: **4 portions**

INGREDIENTS:

- 1 lb chicken thighs
- 1 bell pepper, sliced
- 1 onion, sliced
- 2 cloves garlic, minced
- 1 cup tomatoes, crushed
- 1/2 cup chicken broth
- 1 tsp oregano
- 1 tsp basil
- 2 tbsp olive oil
- Salt and pepper to taste

INSTRUCTIONS:

1. **Brown Chicken:**
   - Sauté chicken in olive oil until browned.
2. **Add Vegetables:**
   - Add bell pepper, onion, and garlic; cook until soft.
3. **Combine Ingredients:**
   - Add tomatoes, broth, oregano, basil, salt, and pepper.
4. **Simmer:**
   - Cover and simmer for 30 minutes.
5. **Serve:**
   - Serve immediately.

NUTRITIONAL INFORMATION (PER SERVING):

- **Calories:** 320
- **Protein:** 25g
- **Carbohydrates:** 12g
- **Fat:** 20g
- **Fiber:** 3g
- **Sodium:** 400mg

Enjoy your healthy and flavorful Chicken Cacciatore!

Chicken Tagine with Olives and Lemons

Prep Time: **10 mins** | Cooking Time: **40 mins**
Yield: **4 portions**

INGREDIENTS:

- 1 lb chicken thighs
- 1 cup green olives
- 1 preserved lemon, sliced
- 1 onion, chopped
- 2 cloves garlic, minced
- 1 tsp cumin
- 1 tsp ginger
- 1 tsp turmeric
- 1 tbsp olive oil
- 2 cups chicken broth
- Salt and pepper to taste
- **Optional:** fresh cilantro

INSTRUCTIONS:

1. **Brown Chicken:**
   - Sauté chicken in olive oil until browned.
2. **Add Aromatics:**
   - Add onion, garlic, cumin, ginger, and turmeric; cook until fragrant.
3. **Combine Ingredients:**
   - Add olives, lemon, broth, salt, and pepper.
4. **Simmer:**
   - Cover and simmer for 30 minutes.
5. **Serve:**
   - Garnish with cilantro if desired. Serve immediately.

NUTRITIONAL INFORMATION (PER SERVING):

- **Calories:** 350
- **Protein:** 28g
- **Carbohydrates:** 8g
- **Fat:** 22g
- **Fiber:** 2g
- **Sodium:** 450mg

Enjoy your healthy and flavorful Chicken Tagine with Olives and Lemons!

Beef and Mushroom Stew

Prep Time: **10 mins** | Cooking Time: **1 hour**
Yield: **4 portions**

INGREDIENTS:

- 1 lb beef, cubed
- 2 cups mushrooms, sliced
- 1 onion, chopped
- 2 cloves garlic, minced
- 2 cups beef broth
- 1 tbsp tomato paste
- 1 tsp thyme
- 1 tsp rosemary
- 2 tbsp olive oil
- Salt and pepper to taste

INSTRUCTIONS:

1. **Brown Beef:**
   - Sauté beef in olive oil until browned.
2. **Add Aromatics:**
   - Add onion, garlic, thyme, and rosemary; cook until fragrant.
3. **Combine Ingredients:**
   - Add mushrooms, tomato paste, broth, salt, and pepper.
4. **Simmer:**
   - Cover and simmer for 1 hour.
5. **Serve:**
   - Serve immediately.

NUTRITIONAL INFORMATION (PER SERVING):

- **Calories:** 350
- **Protein:** 30g
- **Carbohydrates:** 10g
- **Fat:** 20g
- **Fiber:** 2g
- **Sodium:** 400mg

Enjoy your healthy and flavorful Beef and Mushroom Stew!

Herbed Turkey Meatloaf

Prep Time: **10 mins** | Cooking Time: **45 mins**
Yield: **4 portions**

INGREDIENTS:

- 1 lb ground turkey
- 1/2 cup breadcrumbs
- 1 egg
- 1/4 cup onion, chopped
- 2 cloves garlic, minced
- 1 tbsp parsley, chopped
- 1 tsp thyme
- 1 tsp rosemary
- Salt and pepper to taste

INSTRUCTIONS:

1. **Mix Ingredients:**
   - Combine all ingredients in a bowl.
2. **Shape Loaf:**
   - Form into a loaf and place in a baking dish.
3. **Bake:**
   - Bake at 375°F for 45 minutes.
4. **Serve:**
   - Serve immediately.

NUTRITIONAL INFORMATION (PER SERVING):

- **Calories:** 250
- **Protein:** 28g
- **Carbohydrates:** 12g
- **Fat:** 10g
- **Fiber:** 2g
- **Sodium:** 300mg

Enjoy your healthy and flavorful Herbed Turkey Meatloaf!

Beef and Eggplant Casserole

Prep Time: **10 mins** | Cooking Time: **40 mins**
Yield: **4 portions**

INGREDIENTS:

- 1 lb ground beef
- 1 large eggplant, sliced
- 1 onion, chopped
- 2 cloves garlic, minced
- 1 cup tomato sauce
- 1 tsp oregano
- 1 tsp basil
- 2 tbsp olive oil
- Salt and pepper to taste
- **Optional:** grated Parmesan

INSTRUCTIONS:

1. **Cook Beef:**
   - Sauté beef, onion, and garlic in olive oil until browned.
2. **Add Sauce:**
   - Stir in tomato sauce, oregano, basil, salt, and pepper.
3. **Layer Ingredients:**
   - Layer eggplant and beef mixture in a baking dish.
4. **Bake:**
   - Bake at 375°F for 30 minutes. Optional: top with Parmesan.
5. **Serve:**
   - Serve immediately.

NUTRITIONAL INFORMATION (PER SERVING):

- **Calories:** 300
- **Protein:** 25g
- **Carbohydrates:** 12g
- **Fat:** 18g
- **Fiber:** 4g
- **Sodium:** 350mg

Enjoy your healthy and flavorful Beef and Eggplant Casserole!

Mediterranean Beef and Lentil Stew

Prep Time: **10 mins** | Cooking Time: **1 hour**
Yield: **4 portions**

INGREDIENTS:

- 1 lb beef, cubed
- 1 cup lentils
- 1 onion, chopped
- 2 cloves garlic, minced
- 1 cup tomatoes, chopped
- 4 cups beef broth
- 1 tsp cumin
- 1 tsp paprika
- 2 tbsp olive oil
- Salt and pepper to taste

INSTRUCTIONS:

1. **Brown Beef:**
   - Sauté beef in olive oil until browned.
2. **Add Vegetables:**
   - Add onion and garlic; cook until soft.
3. **Combine Ingredients:**
   - Add lentils, tomatoes, cumin, paprika, salt, pepper, and broth.
4. **Simmer:**
   - Cover and simmer for 1 hour.
5. **Serve:**
   - Serve immediately.

NUTRITIONAL INFORMATION (PER SERVING):

- **Calories:** 350
- **Protein:** 28g
- **Carbohydrates:** 20g
- **Fat:** 15g
- **Fiber:** 8g
- **Sodium:** 400mg

Enjoy your healthy and flavorful Mediterranean Beef and Lentil Stew!

Lamb Kebabs with Mint Yogurt Sauce

Prep Time: **15 mins** | Cooking Time: **10 mins**
Yield: **4 portions**

INGREDIENTS:

- 1 lb ground lamb
- 2 cloves garlic, minced
- 1 tsp cumin
- 1 tsp coriander
- Salt and pepper to taste
- Mint Yogurt Sauce:
- 1 cup Greek yogurt
- 2 tbsp fresh mint, chopped
- 1 tbsp lemon juice
- Salt to taste

INSTRUCTIONS:

1. **Prepare Kebabs:**
   Mix lamb, garlic, cumin, coriander, salt, and pepper. Form into kebabs.
2. **Cook Kebabs:**
   Grill or pan-fry kebabs for 10 minutes, turning occasionally.
3. **Make Sauce:**
   Mix yogurt, mint, lemon juice, and salt.
4. **Serve:**
   Serve kebabs with mint yogurt sauce.

NUTRITIONAL INFORMATION (PER SERVING):

- **Calories:** 350
- **Protein:** 25g
- **Carbohydrates:** 6g
- **Fat:** 25g
- **Fiber:** 1g
- **Sodium:** 300mg

Enjoy your healthy and flavorful Lamb Kebabs with Mint Yogurt Sauce!

Greek Lemon Chicken

Prep Time: **10 mins** | Cooking Time: **30 mins**
Yield: **4 portions**

INGREDIENTS:

- 1 lb chicken thighs
- 2 tbsp olive oil
- 1 lemon, juiced
- 2 cloves garlic, minced
- 1 tsp oregano
- Salt and pepper to taste

INSTRUCTIONS:

1. **Marinate Chicken:**
   Mix olive oil, lemon juice, garlic, oregano, salt, and pepper. Marinate chicken for 10 minutes.
2. **Cook Chicken:**
   Sauté chicken in a skillet over medium heat for 30 minutes, turning occasionally.
3. **Serve:**
   Serve immediately.

NUTRITIONAL INFORMATION (PER SERVING):

- **Calories:** 300
- **Protein:** 25g
- **Carbohydrates:** 3g
- **Fat:** 20g
- **Fiber:** 1g
- **Sodium:** 250mg

Enjoy your healthy and flavorful Greek Lemon Chicken!

Chicken and Artichoke Casserole

Prep Time: **10 mins** | Cooking Time: **30 mins**
Yield: **4 portions**

INGREDIENTS:

- 1 lb chicken breasts, cubed
- 1 can artichoke hearts, drained and chopped
- 1 cup spinach, chopped
- 1/2 cup mozzarella, shredded
- 2 cloves garlic, minced
- 2 tbsp olive oil
- Salt and pepper to taste

INSTRUCTIONS:

1. **Cook Chicken:**
   - Sauté chicken and garlic in olive oil until cooked.
2. **Combine Ingredients:**
   - Mix chicken, artichokes, spinach, salt, and pepper in a baking dish. Top with mozzarella.
3. **Bake:**
   - Bake at 375°F for 20 minutes.
4. **Serve:**
   - Serve immediately.

NUTRITIONAL INFORMATION (PER SERVING):

- **Calories:** 300
- **Protein:** 28g
- **Carbohydrates:** 8g
- **Fat:** 18g
- **Fiber:** 3g
- **Sodium:** 350mg

Enjoy your healthy and flavorful Chicken and Artichoke Casserole!

Chicken and Vegetable Skewers

Prep Time: **10 mins** | Cooking Time: **15 mins**
Yield: **4 portions**

INGREDIENTS:

- 1 lb chicken breasts, cubed
- 1 bell pepper, chopped
- 1 zucchini, sliced
- 1 red onion, chopped
- 2 tbsp olive oil
- 1 tbsp lemon juice
- 1 tsp oregano
- Salt and pepper to taste

INSTRUCTIONS:

1. **Marinate Chicken:**
   - Mix olive oil, lemon juice, oregano, salt, and pepper. Marinate chicken for 10 minutes.
2. **Assemble Skewers:**
   - Thread chicken, bell pepper, zucchini, and onion onto skewers.
3. **Cook Skewers:**
   - Grill or broil for 10-15 minutes, turning occasionally.
4. **Serve:**
   - Serve immediately.

NUTRITIONAL INFORMATION (PER SERVING):

- **Calories:** 250
- **Protein:** 25g
- **Carbohydrates:** 8g
- **Fat:** 14g
- **Fiber:** 2g
- **Sodium:** 200mg

Enjoy your healthy and flavorful Chicken and Vegetable Skewers!

Grilled Chicken with Avocado Salsa

Prep Time: **10 mins** | Cooking Time: **15 mins**
Yield: **4 portions**

INGREDIENTS:

- 1 lb chicken breasts
- 1 tbsp olive oil
- Salt and pepper to taste

Avocado Salsa:
- 1 avocado, diced
- 1/2 cup cherry tomatoes, halved
- 1/4 cup red onion, chopped
- 1 tbsp lime juice
- Salt to taste

INSTRUCTIONS:

1. **Grill Chicken:**
   - Season chicken with olive oil, salt, and pepper. Grill for 15 minutes.
2. **Make Salsa:**
   - Combine avocado, tomatoes, onion, lime juice, and salt.
3. **Serve:**
   - Top chicken with avocado salsa and serve immediately.

NUTRITIONAL INFORMATION (PER SERVING):

- **Calories:** 300
- **Protein:** 25g
- **Carbohydrates:** 10g
- **Fat:** 18g
- **Fiber:** 5g
- **Sodium:** 200mg

Enjoy your healthy and flavorful Grilled Chicken with Avocado Salsa!

Honey Mustard Chicken Thighs

Prep Time: **10 mins** | Cooking Time: **25 mins**
Yield: **4 portions**

INGREDIENTS:

- 1 lb chicken thighs
- 2 tbsp honey
- 2 tbsp Dijon mustard
- 1 tbsp olive oil
- Salt and pepper to taste

INSTRUCTIONS:

1. **Prepare Sauce:**
   - Mix honey, mustard, olive oil, salt, and pepper.
2. **Cook Chicken:**
   - Sear chicken thighs in a skillet over medium heat until browned, about 5 minutes per side.
3. **Add Sauce:**
   - Pour sauce over chicken, cover, and simmer for 15 minutes.
4. **Serve:**
   - Serve immediately.

NUTRITIONAL INFORMATION (PER SERVING):

- **Calories:** 350
- **Protein:** 25g
- **Carbohydrates:** 12g
- **Fat:** 20g
- **Fiber:** 0g
- **Sodium:** 300mg

Enjoy your healthy and flavorful Honey Mustard Chicken Thighs!

Lamb Kofta

Prep Time: **10 mins** | Cooking Time: **15 mins**
Yield: **4 portions**

INGREDIENTS:

- 1 lb ground lamb
- 1/4 cup onion, finely chopped
- 2 cloves garlic, minced
- 1 tsp cumin
- 1 tsp coriander
- Salt and pepper to taste
- **Optional:** fresh parsley or mint

INSTRUCTIONS:

1. **Mix Ingredients:**
   - Combine lamb, onion, garlic, cumin, coriander, salt, and pepper. Form into logs or patties.
2. **Cook Kofta:**
   - Grill or pan-fry over medium heat for 15 minutes, turning occasionally.
3. **Serve:**
   - Garnish with parsley or mint if desired. Serve immediately.

NUTRITIONAL INFORMATION (PER SERVING):

- **Calories:** 300
- **Protein:** 20g
- **Carbohydrates:** 2g
- **Fat:** 24g
- **Fiber:** 0g
- **Sodium:** 250mg

Enjoy your healthy and flavorful Lamb Kofta!

Beef and Mushroom Stroganoff

Prep Time: **10 mins** | Cooking Time: **20 mins**
Yield: **4 portions**

INGREDIENTS:

- 1 lb beef strips
- 2 cups mushrooms, sliced
- 1 onion, chopped
- 2 cloves garlic, minced
- 1 cup beef broth
- 1/2 cup Greek yogurt
- 2 tbsp olive oil
- 1 tsp paprika
- Salt and pepper to taste

INSTRUCTIONS:

1. **Cook Beef:**
   - Sauté beef in olive oil until browned. Remove from skillet.
2. **Cook Vegetables:**
   - Sauté onions, garlic, and mushrooms in the same skillet until soft.
3. **Combine Ingredients:**
   - Return beef to skillet, add broth, and paprika. Simmer for 10 minutes.
4. **Add Yogurt:**
   - Stir in Greek yogurt. Season with salt and pepper.
5. **Serve:**
   - Serve immediately.

NUTRITIONAL INFORMATION (PER SERVING):

- **Calories:** 350
- **Protein:** 30g
- **Carbohydrates:** 10g
- **Fat:** 20g
- **Fiber:** 2g
- **Sodium:** 300mg

Enjoy your healthy and flavorful Beef and Mushroom Stroganoff!

CHAPTER 4. MEAT AND POULTRY

CHAPTER 5. FISH AND SEAFOOD

Baked Salmon with Dill and Lemon

Prep Time: **5 mins** | Cooking Time: **15 mins**
Yield: **4 portions**

INGREDIENTS:

- 1 lb salmon fillets
- 1 lemon, sliced
- 2 tbsp fresh dill, chopped
- 2 tbsp olive oil
- Salt and pepper to taste

INSTRUCTIONS:

1. **Prepare Salmon:**
   - Place salmon on a baking sheet. Drizzle with olive oil, and season with salt, pepper, and dill. Top with lemon slices.
2. **Bake:**
   - Bake at 375°F for 15 minutes.
3. **Serve:**
   - Serve immediately.

NUTRITIONAL INFORMATION (PER SERVING):

- **Calories:** 300
- **Protein:** 25g
- **Carbohydrates:** 2g
- **Fat:** 20g
- **Fiber:** 1g
- **Sodium:** 200mg

Enjoy your healthy and flavorful Baked Salmon with Dill and Lemon!

✷ Shrimp Scampi with Garlic and Olive Oil

Prep Time: **5 mins** | Cooking Time: **10 mins**
Yield: **4 portions**

INGREDIENTS:

- 1 lb shrimp, peeled and deveined
- 4 cloves garlic, minced
- 1/4 cup olive oil
- 1/4 cup lemon juice
- 1/4 cup parsley, chopped
- Salt and pepper to taste

INSTRUCTIONS:

1. **Cook Shrimp:**
   - Sauté garlic in olive oil until fragrant. Add shrimp, cook until pink.
2. **Add Lemon:**
   - Stir in lemon juice, salt, and pepper.
3. **Finish:**
   - Sprinkle with parsley. Serve immediately.

NUTRITIONAL INFORMATION (PER SERVING):

- **Calories:** 250
- **Protein:** 20g
- **Carbohydrates:** 2g
- **Fat:** 18g
- **Fiber:** 1g
- **Sodium:** 400mg

Enjoy your healthy and flavorful Shrimp Scampi with Garlic and Olive Oil!

Grilled Swordfish with Capers

Prep Time: **5 mins** | Cooking Time: **10 mins**
Yield: **4 portions**

INGREDIENTS:

- 1 lb swordfish steaks
- 2 tbsp olive oil
- 2 tbsp capers
- 1 lemon, juiced
- Salt and pepper to taste
- **Optional:** fresh parsley

INSTRUCTIONS:

1. **Prepare Swordfish:**
   - Brush swordfish with olive oil, season with salt and pepper.
2. **Grill Swordfish:**
   - Grill for 5 minutes per side.
3. **Add Capers:**
   - Drizzle with lemon juice and top with capers. Garnish with parsley if desired.
4. **Serve:**
   - Serve immediately.

NUTRITIONAL INFORMATION (PER SERVING):

- **Calories:** 250
- **Protein:** 30g
- **Carbohydrates:** 2g
- **Fat:** 12g
- **Fiber:** 1g
- **Sodium:** 250mg

Enjoy your healthy and flavorful Grilled Swordfish with Capers!

Garlic Butter Shrimp with Zoodles

Prep Time: **5 mins** | Cooking Time: **10 mins**
Yield: **4 portions**

INGREDIENTS:

- 1 lb shrimp, peeled and deveined
- 4 zucchinis, spiralized
- 4 cloves garlic, minced
- 2 tbsp butter
- 1 tbsp olive oil
- Salt and pepper to taste
- **Optional:** parsley, lemon juice

INSTRUCTIONS:

1. **Cook Shrimp:**
   - Sauté garlic in butter and olive oil until fragrant. Add shrimp, cook until pink.
2. **Add Zoodles:**
   - Stir in zoodles, cook for 2-3 minutes. Season with salt and pepper.
3. **Finish:**
   - Garnish with parsley and lemon juice if desired. Serve immediately.

NUTRITIONAL INFORMATION (PER SERVING):

- **Calories:** 200
- **Protein:** 20g
- **Carbohydrates:** 6g
- **Fat:** 12g
- **Fiber:** 2g
- **Sodium:** 300mg

Enjoy your healthy and flavorful Garlic Butter Shrimp with Zoodles!

Grilled Octopus with Lemon and Olive Oil

Prep Time: **5 mins** | Cooking Time: **40 mins**
Yield: **4 portions**

INGREDIENTS:

- 1 lb octopus
- 2 tbsp olive oil
- 1 lemon, juiced
- Salt and pepper to taste
- **Optional:** fresh parsley

INSTRUCTIONS:

1. **Boil Octopus:**
   Boil octopus for 30 minutes. Drain and cool.
2. **Grill Octopus:**
   Brush with olive oil, grill for 5 minutes per side.
3. **Add Lemon:**
   Drizzle with lemon juice, season with salt and pepper. Garnish with parsley if desired.
4. **Serve:**
   Serve immediately.

NUTRITIONAL INFORMATION (PER SERVING):

- **Calories:** 200
- **Protein:** 30g
- **Carbohydrates:** 2g
- **Fat:** 8g
- **Fiber:** 1g
- **Sodium:** 250mg

Enjoy your healthy and flavorful Grilled Octopus with Lemon and Olive Oil!

Mediterranean Mussels in White Wine Sauce

Prep Time: **5 mins** | Cooking Time: **10 mins**
Yield: **4 portions**

INGREDIENTS:

- 2 lbs mussels, cleaned
- 1 cup white wine
- 4 cloves garlic, minced
- 2 tbsp olive oil
- 1 lemon, juiced
- Salt and pepper to taste
- **Optional:** fresh parsley

INSTRUCTIONS:

1. **Cook Garlic:**
   Sauté garlic in olive oil until fragrant.
2. **Add Mussels:**
   Add mussels, white wine, and lemon juice. Cover and cook until mussels open, about 5 minutes.
3. **Season:**
   Season with salt and pepper. Garnish with parsley if desired.
4. **Serve:**
   Serve immediately.

NUTRITIONAL INFORMATION (PER SERVING):

- **Calories:** 250
- **Protein:** 18g
- **Carbohydrates:** 8g
- **Fat:** 10g
- **Fiber:** 1g
- **Sodium:** 400mg

Enjoy your healthy and flavorful Mediterranean Mussels in White Wine Sauce!

Pan-Seared Scallops with Herb Butter

Prep Time: **5 mins** | Cooking Time: **10 mins**
Yield: **4 portions**

INGREDIENTS:

- 1 lb scallops
- 2 tbsp butter
- 2 cloves garlic, minced
- 2 tbsp fresh herbs (parsley, thyme), chopped
- 1 tbsp olive oil
- Salt and pepper to taste

INSTRUCTIONS:

1. **Sear Scallops:**
   - Heat olive oil in a skillet. Season scallops with salt and pepper, sear for 2-3 minutes per side. Remove from skillet.
2. **Make Herb Butter:**
   - In the same skillet, melt butter, add garlic and herbs, cook until fragrant.
3. **Combine:**
   - Return scallops to skillet, toss in herb butter.
4. **Serve:**
   - Serve immediately.

NUTRITIONAL INFORMATION (PER SERVING):

- **Calories:** 200
- **Protein:** 20g
- **Carbohydrates:** 2g
- **Fat:** 12g
- **Fiber:** 0g
- **Sodium:** 300mg

Enjoy your healthy and flavorful Pan-Seared Scallops with Herb Butter!

Seafood Risotto with Saffron

Prep Time: **10 mins** | Cooking Time: **30 mins**
Yield: **4 portions**

INGREDIENTS:

- 1 cup arborio rice
- 1/2 lb shrimp, peeled
- 1/2 lb mussels, cleaned
- 1 onion, chopped
- 2 cloves garlic, minced
- 4 cups chicken broth
- 1 cup white wine
- 1 pinch saffron
- 2 tbsp olive oil
- Salt and pepper to taste
- **Optional:** parsley

INSTRUCTIONS:

1. **Cook Onion:**
   - Sauté onion and garlic in olive oil until soft.
2. **Add Rice:**
   - Stir in rice, cook until translucent. Add saffron and wine, cook until absorbed.
3. **Add Broth:**
   - Gradually add broth, stirring constantly until absorbed.
4. **Add Seafood:**
   - Add shrimp and mussels, cook until seafood is done.
5. **Serve:**
   - Season with salt and pepper. Garnish with parsley if desired. Serve immediately.

NUTRITIONAL INFORMATION (PER SERVING):

- **Calories:** 350
- **Protein:** 22g
- **Carbohydrates:** 40g
- **Fat:** 10g
- **Fiber:** 2g
- **Sodium:** 400mg

Enjoy your healthy and flavorful Seafood Risotto with Saffron!

Grilled Shrimp with Mango Salsa

Prep Time: **10 mins** | Cooking Time: **10 mins**
Yield: **4 portions**

INGREDIENTS:

- 1 lb shrimp, peeled and deveined
- 2 tbsp olive oil
- Salt and pepper to taste
- Mango Salsa:
- 1 mango, diced
- 1/4 cup red onion, chopped
- 1/4 cup cilantro, chopped
- 1 tbsp lime juice
- Salt to taste

INSTRUCTIONS:

1. **Grill Shrimp:**
   Toss shrimp with olive oil, salt, and pepper. Grill for 2-3 minutes per side.
2. **Make Salsa:**
   Mix mango, onion, cilantro, lime juice, and salt.
3. **Serve:**
   Top shrimp with mango salsa. Serve immediately.

NUTRITIONAL INFORMATION (PER SERVING):

- **Calories:** 250
- **Protein:** 20g
- **Carbohydrates:** 15g
- **Fat:** 12g
- **Fiber:** 2g
- **Sodium:** 300mg

Enjoy your healthy and flavorful Grilled Shrimp with Mango Salsa!

Baked Tilapia with Spinach and Feta

Prep Time: **10 mins** | Cooking Time: **20 mins**
Yield: **4 portions**

INGREDIENTS:

- 4 tilapia fillets
- 2 cups spinach, chopped
- 1/2 cup feta cheese, crumbled
- 2 tbsp olive oil
- 1 lemon, sliced
- Salt and pepper to taste

INSTRUCTIONS:

1. **Prepare Tilapia:**
   Place tilapia on a baking sheet. Drizzle with olive oil, season with salt and pepper.
2. **Add Toppings:**
   Top with spinach and feta. Arrange lemon slices on top.
3. **Bake:**
   Bake at 375°F for 20 minutes.
4. **Serve:**
   Serve immediately.

NUTRITIONAL INFORMATION (PER SERVING):

- **Calories:** 300
- **Protein:** 30g
- **Carbohydrates:** 4g
- **Fat:** 18g
- **Fiber:** 1g
- **Sodium:** 350mg

Enjoy your healthy and flavorful Baked Tilapia with Spinach and Feta!

Grilled Mackerel with Citrus Salsa

Prep Time: **10 mins** | Cooking Time: **10 mins**
Yield: **4 portions**

INGREDIENTS:

- 4 mackerel fillets
- 2 tbsp olive oil
- Salt and pepper to taste

Citrus Salsa:
- 1 orange, diced
- 1 grapefruit, diced
- 1/4 cup red onion, chopped
- 1 tbsp lime juice
- Salt to taste

INSTRUCTIONS:

1. **Grill Mackerel:**
   - Brush fillets with olive oil, season with salt and pepper. Grill for 5 minutes per side.
2. **Make Salsa:**
   - Combine orange, grapefruit, onion, lime juice, and salt.
3. **Serve:**
   - Top mackerel with citrus salsa. Serve immediately.

NUTRITIONAL INFORMATION (PER SERVING):

- **Calories:** 280
- **Protein:** 25g
- **Carbohydrates:** 10g
- **Fat:** 16g
- **Fiber:** 2g
- **Sodium:** 300mg

Enjoy your healthy and flavorful Grilled Mackerel with Citrus Salsa!

Seared Tuna with Sesame and Soy

Prep Time: **5 mins** | Cooking Time: **5 mins**
Yield: **4 portions**

INGREDIENTS:

- 4 tuna steaks
- 2 tbsp soy sauce
- 2 tbsp sesame oil
- 1 tbsp olive oil
- 1 tbsp sesame seeds
- Salt and pepper to taste

INSTRUCTIONS:

1. **Marinate Tuna:**
   - Marinate tuna in soy sauce, sesame oil, salt, and pepper for 5 minutes.
2. **Sear Tuna:**
   - Sear in olive oil over high heat, 2 minutes per side. Sprinkle with sesame seeds.
3. **Serve:**
   - Serve immediately.

NUTRITIONAL INFORMATION (PER SERVING):

- **Calories:** 300
- **Protein:** 30g
- **Carbohydrates:** 2g
- **Fat:** 20g
- **Fiber:** 1g
- **Sodium:** 400mg

Enjoy your healthy and flavorful Seared Tuna with Sesame and Soy!

Grilled Calamari with Lemon and Parsley

Prep Time: **10 mins** | Cooking Time: **5 mins**
Yield: **4 portions**

INGREDIENTS:

- 1 lb calamari, cleaned
- 2 tbsp olive oil
- 1 lemon, juiced
- 2 tbsp parsley, chopped
- Salt and pepper to taste

INSTRUCTIONS:

1. **Marinate Calamari:**
   - Toss calamari with olive oil, lemon juice, salt, and pepper.
2. **Grill Calamari:**
   - Grill over high heat for 2-3 minutes per side.
3. **Serve:**
   - Sprinkle with parsley and serve immediately.

NUTRITIONAL INFORMATION (PER SERVING):

- **Calories:** 150
- **Protein:** 20g
- **Carbohydrates:** 2g
- **Fat:** 7g
- **Fiber:** 1g
- **Sodium:** 200mg

Enjoy your healthy and flavorful Grilled Calamari with Lemon and Parsley!

Roasted Sea Bass with Olives and Tomatoes

Prep Time: **10 mins** | Cooking Time: **20 mins**
Yield: **4 portions**

INGREDIENTS:

- 1 lb sea bass fillets
- 1 cup cherry tomatoes, halved
- 1/2 cup olives, sliced
- 2 tbsp olive oil
- 1 lemon, sliced
- Salt and pepper to taste
- **Optional:** fresh thyme

INSTRUCTIONS:

1. **Prepare Fish:**
   - Place sea bass on a baking sheet. Drizzle with olive oil, salt, and pepper.
2. **Add Toppings:**
   - Top with tomatoes, olives, lemon slices, and thyme.
3. **Roast:**
   - Roast at 375°F for 20 minutes.
4. **Serve:**
   - Serve immediately.

NUTRITIONAL INFORMATION (PER SERVING):

- **Calories:** 250
- **Protein:** 25g
- **Carbohydrates:** 5g
- **Fat:** 15g
- **Fiber:** 2g
- **Sodium:** 350mg

Enjoy your healthy and flavorful Roasted Sea Bass with Olives and Tomatoes!

CHAPTER 6. VEGETABLES AND SIDES

Roasted Eggplant with Tahini

Prep Time: **10 mins** | Cooking Time: **30 mins**
Yield: **4 portions**

INGREDIENTS:

- 2 eggplants, sliced
- 2 tbsp olive oil
- 1/4 cup tahini
- 2 tbsp lemon juice
- 2 cloves garlic, minced
- Salt and pepper to taste
- **Optional:** fresh parsley

INSTRUCTIONS:

1. **Roast Eggplant:**
   - Toss eggplant with olive oil, salt, and pepper. Roast at 400°F for 30 minutes.
2. **Make Tahini Sauce:**
   - Mix tahini, lemon juice, garlic, salt, and water until smooth.
3. **Serve:**
   - Drizzle eggplant with tahini sauce and garnish with parsley.

NUTRITIONAL INFORMATION (PER SERVING):

- **Calories:** 200
- **Protein:** 3g
- **Carbohydrates:** 15g
- **Fat:** 15g
- **Fiber:** 7g
- **Sodium:** 200mg

Enjoy your healthy and flavorful Roasted Eggplant with Tahini!

Grilled Zucchini with Lemon and Basil

Prep Time: **5 mins** | Cooking Time: **10 mins**
Yield: **4 portions**

INGREDIENTS:

- 4 zucchinis, sliced
- 2 tbsp olive oil
- 1 lemon, juiced
- 2 tbsp fresh basil, chopped
- Salt and pepper to taste

INSTRUCTIONS:

1. **Grill Zucchini:**
   - Toss zucchini with olive oil, salt, and pepper. Grill for 3-4 minutes per side.
2. **Add Lemon and Basil:**
   - Drizzle with lemon juice and sprinkle with basil.
3. **Serve:**
   - Serve immediately.

NUTRITIONAL INFORMATION (PER SERVING):

- **Calories:** 80
- **Protein:** 2g
- **Carbohydrates:** 7g
- **Fat:** 6g
- **Fiber:** 2g
- **Sodium:** 150mg

Enjoy your healthy and flavorful Grilled Zucchini with Lemon and Basil!

Baked Feta with Tomatoes and Olives

Prep Time: **5 mins** | Cooking Time: **20 mins**
Yield: **4 portions**

INGREDIENTS:

- 8 oz feta cheese
- 1 cup cherry tomatoes, halved
- 1/2 cup olives, pitted
- 2 tbsp olive oil
- 1 tsp oregano
- Salt and pepper to taste

INSTRUCTIONS:

1. **Prepare Dish:**
   - Place feta in a baking dish. Top with tomatoes, olives, olive oil, oregano, salt, and pepper.
2. **Bake:**
   - Bake at 375°F for 20 minutes.
3. **Serve:**
   - Serve immediately.

NUTRITIONAL INFORMATION (PER SERVING):

- **Calories:** 200
- **Protein:** 7g
- **Carbohydrates:** 5g
- **Fat:** 18g
- **Fiber:** 2g
- **Sodium:** 500mg

Enjoy your healthy and flavorful Baked Feta with Tomatoes and Olives!

Ratatouille

Prep Time: **10 mins** | Cooking Time: **30 mins**
Yield: **4 portions**

INGREDIENTS:

- 1 eggplant, diced
- 2 zucchinis, diced
- 1 bell pepper, diced
- 1 onion, chopped
- 2 tomatoes, chopped
- 2 cloves garlic, minced
- 2 tbsp olive oil
- 1 tsp thyme
- Salt and pepper to taste

INSTRUCTIONS:

1. **Sauté Vegetables:**
   - Sauté onion and garlic in olive oil until soft. Add eggplant, zucchini, and bell pepper. Cook until tender.
2. **Add Tomatoes:**
   - Stir in tomatoes, thyme, salt, and pepper. Simmer for 20 minutes.
3. **Serve:**
   - Serve immediately.

NUTRITIONAL INFORMATION (PER SERVING):

- **Calories:** 150
- **Protein:** 3g
- **Carbohydrates:** 15g
- **Fat:** 10g
- **Fiber:** 5g
- **Sodium:** 200mg

Enjoy your healthy and flavorful Ratatouille!

Mediterranean Mashed Potatoes

Prep Time: **10 mins** | Cooking Time: **20 mins**
Yield: **4 portions**

INGREDIENTS:

- 2 lbs potatoes, peeled and diced
- 1/4 cup olive oil
- 1/4 cup feta cheese, crumbled
- 2 cloves garlic, minced
- 1/4 cup fresh parsley, chopped
- Salt and pepper to taste

INSTRUCTIONS:

1. **Boil Potatoes:**
   - Boil potatoes until tender, about 15 minutes. Drain.
2. **Mash Potatoes:**
   - Mash potatoes with olive oil, garlic, feta, salt, and pepper.
3. **Add Herbs:**
   - Stir in parsley.
4. **Serve:**
   - Serve immediately.

NUTRITIONAL INFORMATION (PER SERVING):

- **Calories:** 250
- **Protein:** 4g
- **Carbohydrates:** 35g
- **Fat:** 12g
- **Fiber:** 4g
- **Sodium:** 300mg

Enjoy your healthy and flavorful Mediterranean Mashed Potatoes!

Grilled Asparagus with Parmesan

Prep Time: **5 mins** | Cooking Time: **10 mins**
Yield: **4 portions**

INGREDIENTS:

- 1 lb asparagus, trimmed
- 2 tbsp olive oil
- 1/4 cup Parmesan cheese, grated
- Salt and pepper to taste

INSTRUCTIONS:

1. **Prepare Asparagus:**
   - Toss asparagus with olive oil, salt, and pepper.
2. **Grill:**
   - Grill over medium heat for 8-10 minutes, turning occasionally.
3. **Add Parmesan:**
   - Sprinkle with Parmesan cheese.
4. **Serve:**
   - Serve immediately.

NUTRITIONAL INFORMATION (PER SERVING):

- **Calories:** 120
- **Protein:** 4g
- **Carbohydrates:** 5g
- **Fat:** 10g
- **Fiber:** 2g
- **Sodium:** 200mg

Enjoy your healthy and flavorful Grilled Asparagus with Parmesan!

Stuffed Mushrooms with Spinach and Feta

Prep Time: **10 mins** | Cooking Time: **15 mins**
Yield: **4 portions**

INGREDIENTS:

- 12 large mushrooms, stems removed
- 1 cup spinach, chopped
- 1/2 cup feta cheese, crumbled
- 2 tbsp olive oil
- 1 clove garlic, minced
- Salt and pepper to taste

INSTRUCTIONS:

1. **Prepare Filling:**
   - Sauté spinach and garlic in olive oil until wilted. Mix in feta, salt, and pepper.
2. **Stuff Mushrooms:**
   - Fill mushroom caps with the spinach mixture.
3. **Bake:**
   - Bake at 375°F for 15 minutes.
4. **Serve:**
   - Serve immediately.

NUTRITIONAL INFORMATION (PER SERVING):

- **Calories:** 120
- **Protein:** 5g
- **Carbohydrates:** 5g
- **Fat:** 10g
- **Fiber:** 2g
- **Sodium:** 250mg

Enjoy your healthy and flavorful Stuffed Mushrooms with Spinach and Feta!

Roasted Butternut Squash with Sage

Prep Time: **10 mins** | Cooking Time: **30 mins**
Yield: **4 portions**

INGREDIENTS:

- 1 butternut squash, peeled and cubed
- 2 tbsp olive oil
- 1 tbsp fresh sage, chopped
- Salt and pepper to taste

INSTRUCTIONS:

1. **Prepare Squash:**
   - Toss squash with olive oil, sage, salt, and pepper.
2. **Roast:**
   - Roast at 400°F for 30 minutes, turning halfway.
3. **Serve:**
   - Serve immediately.

NUTRITIONAL INFORMATION (PER SERVING):

- **Calories:** 150
- **Protein:** 2g
- **Carbohydrates:** 20g
- **Fat:** 7g
- **Fiber:** 4g
- **Sodium:** 200mg

Enjoy your healthy and flavorful Roasted Butternut Squash with Sage!

Baked Zucchini Chips

Prep Time: **10 mins** | Cooking Time: **20 mins**
Yield: **4 portions**

INGREDIENTS:

- 2 zucchinis, thinly sliced
- 2 tbsp olive oil
- 1/4 cup Parmesan cheese, grated
- Salt and pepper to taste

INSTRUCTIONS:

1. **Prepare Zucchini:**
   - Toss zucchini slices with olive oil, Parmesan, salt, and pepper.
2. **Bake:**
   - Arrange on a baking sheet. Bake at 425°F for 20 minutes, turning once.
3. **Serve:**
   - Serve immediately.

NUTRITIONAL INFORMATION (PER SERVING):

- **Calories:** 100
- **Protein:** 4g
- **Carbohydrates:** 5g
- **Fat:** 8g
- **Fiber:** 1g
- **Sodium:** 150mg

Enjoy your healthy and flavorful Baked Zucchini Chips!

Mediterranean Quinoa Stuffed Tomatoes

Prep Time: **10 mins** | Cooking Time: **20 mins**
Yield: **4 portions**

INGREDIENTS:

- 4 large tomatoes
- 1 cup cooked quinoa
- 1/4 cup feta cheese, crumbled
- 1/4 cup olives, chopped
- 2 tbsp parsley, chopped
- 1 tbsp olive oil
- Salt and pepper to taste

INSTRUCTIONS:

1. **Prepare Tomatoes:**
   - Hollow out tomatoes.
2. **Mix Filling:**
   - Combine quinoa, feta, olives, parsley, olive oil, salt, and pepper.
3. **Stuff Tomatoes:**
   - Fill tomatoes with quinoa mixture.
4. **Bake:**
   - Bake at 375°F for 20 minutes.
5. **Serve:**
   - Serve immediately.

NUTRITIONAL INFORMATION (PER SERVING):

- **Calories:** 150
- **Protein:** 5g
- **Carbohydrates:** 15g
- **Fat:** 8g
- **Fiber:** 3g
- **Sodium:** 200mg

Enjoy your healthy and flavorful Mediterranean Quinoa Stuffed Tomatoes!

Roasted Beet Salad with Feta

Prep Time: **10 mins** | Cooking Time: **30 mins**
Yield: **4 portions**

INGREDIENTS:

- 4 beets, roasted and diced
- 1/4 cup feta cheese, crumbled
- 2 tbsp olive oil
- 1 tbsp balsamic vinegar
- Salt and pepper to taste
- **Optional:** fresh mint or parsley

INSTRUCTIONS:

1. **Roast Beets:**
   - Roast beets at 400°F for 30 minutes. Cool and dice.
2. **Combine Ingredients:**
   - Toss beets with olive oil, balsamic vinegar, salt, and pepper. Top with feta and optional herbs.
3. **Serve:**
   - Serve immediately.

NUTRITIONAL INFORMATION (PER SERVING):

- **Calories:** 150
- **Protein:** 3g
- **Carbohydrates:** 15g
- **Fat:** 9g
- **Fiber:** 3g
- **Sodium:** 200mg

Enjoy your healthy and flavorful Roasted Beet Salad with Feta!

Stuffed Acorn Squash with Wild Rice

Prep Time: **10 mins** | Cooking Time: **40 mins**
Yield: **4 portions**

INGREDIENTS:

- 2 acorn squashes, halved and seeded
- 1 cup cooked wild rice
- 1/4 cup cranberries
- 1/4 cup pecans, chopped
- 1/4 cup parsley, chopped
- 2 tbsp olive oil
- Salt and pepper to taste

INSTRUCTIONS:

1. **Roast Squash:**
   - Brush squash halves with olive oil, salt, and pepper. Roast at 400°F for 30 minutes.
2. **Prepare Filling:**
   - Mix wild rice, cranberries, pecans, and parsley. Season with salt and pepper.
3. **Stuff Squash:**
   - Fill roasted squash with the rice mixture.
4. **Bake:**
   - Bake for an additional 10 minutes.
5. **Serve:**
   - Serve immediately.

NUTRITIONAL INFORMATION (PER SERVING):

- **Calories:** 250
- **Protein:** 4g
- **Carbohydrates:** 35g
- **Fat:** 12g
- **Fiber:** 6g
- **Sodium:** 200mg

Enjoy your healthy and flavorful Stuffed Acorn Squash with Wild Rice!

Roasted Fennel with Parmesan

Prep Time: **5 mins** | Cooking Time: **25 mins**
Yield: **4 portions**

INGREDIENTS:

- 2 fennel bulbs, sliced
- 2 tbsp olive oil
- 1/4 cup Parmesan cheese, grated
- Salt and pepper to taste

INSTRUCTIONS:

1. **Prepare Fennel:**
   - Toss fennel slices with olive oil, salt, and pepper.
2. **Roast:**
   - Roast at 400°F for 20 minutes.
3. **Add Parmesan:**
   - Sprinkle with Parmesan and roast for 5 more minutes.
4. **Serve:**
   - Serve immediately.

NUTRITIONAL INFORMATION (PER SERVING):

- **Calories:** 130
- **Protein:** 4g
- **Carbohydrates:** 7g
- **Fat:** 10g
- **Fiber:** 3g
- **Sodium:** 180mg

Enjoy your healthy and flavorful Roasted Fennel with Parmesan!

Baked Stuffed Eggplant Rolls

Prep Time: **10 mins** | Cooking Time: **25 mins**
Yield: **4 portions**

INGREDIENTS:

- 2 eggplants, sliced lengthwise
- 1 cup ricotta cheese
- 1/2 cup spinach, chopped
- 1/4 cup Parmesan cheese, grated
- 1 cup marinara sauce
- 2 tbsp olive oil
- Salt and pepper to taste

INSTRUCTIONS:

1. **Prepare Eggplant:**
   - Brush eggplant slices with olive oil, season with salt and pepper. Roast at 375°F for 10 minutes.
2. **Mix Filling:**
   - Combine ricotta, spinach, Parmesan, salt, and pepper.
3. **Stuff Eggplant:**
   - Place filling on eggplant slices, roll up, and secure with toothpicks.
4. **Bake:**
   - Arrange in a baking dish, top with marinara sauce, and bake for 15 minutes.
5. **Serve:**
   - Serve immediately.

NUTRITIONAL INFORMATION (PER SERVING):

- **Calories:** 200
- **Protein:** 8g
- **Carbohydrates:** 15g
- **Fat:** 12g
- **Fiber:** 5g
- **Sodium:** 250mg

Enjoy your healthy and flavorful Baked Stuffed Eggplant Rolls!

CHAPTER 7. VEGETARIAN MAINS

Eggplant Parmesan

Prep Time: **10 mins** | Cooking Time: **30 mins**
Yield: **4 portions**

INGREDIENTS:

- 2 eggplants, sliced
- 2 cups marinara sauce
- 1 cup mozzarella cheese, shredded
- 1/2 cup Parmesan cheese, grated
- 1/4 cup basil, chopped
- 2 tbsp olive oil
- Salt and pepper to taste

INSTRUCTIONS:

1. **Prepare Eggplant:**
   - Brush slices with olive oil, season with salt and pepper. Roast at 375°F for 20 minutes.
2. **Assemble:**
   - Layer eggplant, marinara sauce, mozzarella, and Parmesan in a baking dish.
3. **Bake:**
   - Bake at 375°F for 10 minutes until cheese is melted and bubbly.
4. **Serve:**
   - Garnish with basil and serve immediately.

NUTRITIONAL INFORMATION (PER SERVING):

- **Calories:** 300
- **Protein:** 15g
- **Carbohydrates:** 25g
- **Fat:** 18g
- **Fiber:** 6g
- **Sodium:** 450mg

Enjoy your healthy and flavorful Eggplant Parmesan!

Spinach and Ricotta Stuffed Peppers

Prep Time: **10 mins** | Cooking Time: **20 mins**
Yield: **4 portions**

INGREDIENTS:

- 4 bell peppers, halved and seeded
- 1 cup ricotta cheese
- 1 cup spinach, chopped
- 1/4 cup Parmesan cheese, grated
- 1 clove garlic, minced
- 1 tbsp olive oil
- Salt and pepper to taste

INSTRUCTIONS:

1. **Prepare Filling:**
   - Mix ricotta, spinach, Parmesan, garlic, salt, and pepper.
2. **Stuff Peppers:**
   - Fill bell pepper halves with the mixture.
3. **Bake:**
   - Drizzle with olive oil, bake at 375°F for 20 minutes.
4. **Serve:**
   - Serve immediately.

NUTRITIONAL INFORMATION (PER SERVING):

- **Calories:** 200
- **Protein:** 10g
- **Carbohydrates:** 10g
- **Fat:** 14g
- **Fiber:** 2g
- **Sodium:** 300mg

Enjoy your healthy and flavorful Spinach and Ricotta Stuffed Peppers!

Chickpea and Spinach Stew

Prep Time: **10 mins** | Cooking Time: **20 mins**
Yield: **4 portions**

INGREDIENTS:

- 1 can chickpeas, drained
- 4 cups spinach, chopped
- 1 onion, chopped
- 2 cloves garlic, minced
- 2 cups vegetable broth
- 1 tbsp olive oil
- 1 tsp cumin
- Salt and pepper to taste

INSTRUCTIONS:

1. **Sauté Aromatics:**
   - Sauté onion and garlic in olive oil until soft.
2. **Add Ingredients:**
   - Add chickpeas, spinach, broth, cumin, salt, and pepper. Simmer for 15 minutes.
3. **Serve:**
   - Serve immediately.

NUTRITIONAL INFORMATION (PER SERVING):

- **Calories:** 180
- **Protein:** 8g
- **Carbohydrates:** 25g
- **Fat:** 6g
- **Fiber:** 7g
- **Sodium:** 300mg

Enjoy your healthy and flavorful Chickpea and Spinach Stew!

Mediterranean Vegetable Stir-Fry

Prep Time: **10 mins** | Cooking Time: **10 mins**
Yield: **4 portions**

INGREDIENTS:

- 1 zucchini, sliced
- 1 bell pepper, sliced
- 1 onion, sliced
- 1 cup cherry tomatoes, halved
- 2 cloves garlic, minced
- 2 tbsp olive oil
- 1 tsp oregano
- Salt and pepper to taste

INSTRUCTIONS:

1. **Sauté Vegetables:**
   - Heat olive oil in a skillet. Sauté garlic until fragrant.
2. **Add Vegetables:**
   - Add zucchini, bell pepper, and onion. Cook for 5 minutes.
3. **Finish:**
   - Add cherry tomatoes, oregano, salt, and pepper. Cook for another 5 minutes.
4. **Serve:**
   - Serve immediately.

NUTRITIONAL INFORMATION (PER SERVING):

- **Calories:** 120
- **Protein:** 2g
- **Carbohydrates:** 10g
- **Fat:** 9g
- **Fiber:** 3g
- **Sodium:** 200mg

Enjoy your healthy and flavorful Mediterranean Vegetable Stir-Fry!

Lentil and Vegetable Shepherd's Pie

Prep Time: **10 mins** | Cooking Time: **30 mins**
Yield: **4 portions**

INGREDIENTS:

- 1 cup lentils, cooked
- 1 onion, chopped
- 2 carrots, diced
- 1 cup peas
- 2 cloves garlic, minced
- 2 cups vegetable broth
- 4 cups mashed potatoes
- 2 tbsp olive oil
- 1 tsp thyme
- Salt and pepper to taste

INSTRUCTIONS:

1. **Sauté Vegetables:**
   - Sauté onion, garlic, and carrots in olive oil until soft.
2. **Add Lentils:**
   - Add cooked lentils, peas, broth, thyme, salt, and pepper. Simmer for 10 minutes.
3. **Assemble Pie:**
   - Transfer mixture to a baking dish, top with mashed potatoes.
4. **Bake:**
   - Bake at 375°F for 20 minutes.
5. **Serve:**
   - Serve immediately.

NUTRITIONAL INFORMATION (PER SERVING):

- **Calories:** 300
- **Protein:** 10g
- **Carbohydrates:** 50g
- **Fat:** 8g
- **Fiber:** 12g
- **Sodium:** 400mg

Enjoy your healthy and flavorful Lentil and Vegetable Shepherd's Pie!

Stuffed Acorn Squash with Quinoa

Prep Time: **10 mins** | Cooking Time: **40 mins**
Yield: **4 portions**

INGREDIENTS:

- 2 acorn squashes, halved and seeded
- 1 cup cooked quinoa
- 1/4 cup cranberries
- 1/4 cup chopped nuts (optional)
- 1/4 cup parsley, chopped
- 2 tbsp olive oil
- Salt and pepper to taste

INSTRUCTIONS:

1. **Roast Squash:**
   - Brush squash halves with olive oil, salt, and pepper. Roast at 400°F for 30 minutes.
2. **Prepare Filling:**
   - Mix quinoa, cranberries, nuts, parsley, salt, and pepper.
3. **Stuff Squash:**
   - Fill roasted squash with quinoa mixture.
4. **Bake:**
   - Bake for an additional 10 minutes.
5. **Serve:**
   - Serve immediately.

NUTRITIONAL INFORMATION (PER SERVING):

- **Calories:** 220
- **Protein:** 5g
- **Carbohydrates:** 35g
- **Fat:** 8g
- **Fiber:** 6g
- **Sodium:** 200mg

Enjoy your healthy and flavorful Stuffed Acorn Squash with Quinoa!

Vegetable Paella

Prep Time: **10 mins** | Cooking Time: **30 mins**
Yield: **4 portions**

INGREDIENTS:

- 1 cup arborio rice
- 1 onion, chopped
- 1 bell pepper, chopped
- 1 zucchini, chopped
- 1 cup peas
- 2 cloves garlic, minced
- 4 cups vegetable broth
- 1 tsp paprika
- 1/2 tsp saffron
- 2 tbsp olive oil
- Salt and pepper to taste

INSTRUCTIONS:

1. **Sauté Vegetables:**
   - Sauté onion, garlic, bell pepper, and zucchini in olive oil until soft.
2. **Add Rice:**
   - Add rice, paprika, saffron, salt, and pepper. Stir for 2 minutes.
3. **Cook Rice:**
   - Add broth and peas. Simmer until liquid is absorbed, about 20 minutes.
4. **Serve:**
   - Serve immediately.

NUTRITIONAL INFORMATION (PER SERVING):

- **Calories:** 250
- **Protein:** 6g
- **Carbohydrates:** 45g
- **Fat:** 6g
- **Fiber:** 5g
- **Sodium:** 300mg

Enjoy your healthy and flavorful Vegetable Paella!

Greek Style Lentil Soup

Prep Time: **10 mins** | Cooking Time: **30 mins**
Yield: **4 portions**

INGREDIENTS:

- 1 cup lentils
- 1 onion, chopped
- 2 carrots, diced
- 2 cloves garlic, minced
- 4 cups vegetable broth
- 1 can diced tomatoes
- 1 tsp oregano
- 2 tbsp olive oil
- Salt and pepper to taste
- **Optional:** lemon wedges

INSTRUCTIONS:

1. **Sauté Vegetables:**
   - Sauté onion, garlic, and carrots in olive oil until soft.
2. **Add Ingredients:**
   - Add lentils, broth, tomatoes, oregano, salt, and pepper. Simmer for 30 minutes.
3. **Serve:**
   - Serve with lemon wedges if desired.

NUTRITIONAL INFORMATION (PER SERVING):

- **Calories:** 200
- **Protein:** 10g
- **Carbohydrates:** 30g
- **Fat:** 5g
- **Fiber:** 10g
- **Sodium:** 300mg

Enjoy your healthy and flavorful Greek Style Lentil Soup!

Mediterranean Vegetable Casserole

Prep Time: **10 mins** | Cooking Time: **30 mins**
Yield: **4 portions**

INGREDIENTS:

- 1 eggplant, diced
- 1 zucchini, sliced
- 1 bell pepper, chopped
- 1 onion, chopped
- 2 cloves garlic, minced
- 1 can diced tomatoes
- 1 tsp oregano
- 2 tbsp olive oil
- Salt and pepper to taste
- **Optional:** Parmesan cheese

INSTRUCTIONS:

1. **Sauté Vegetables:**
   - Sauté onion, garlic, eggplant, zucchini, and bell pepper in olive oil until soft.
2. **Combine:**
   - Add tomatoes, oregano, salt, and pepper. Simmer for 10 minutes.
3. **Bake:**
   - Transfer to a baking dish, top with Parmesan if desired. Bake at 375°F for 20 minutes.
4. **Serve:**
   - Serve immediately.

NUTRITIONAL INFORMATION (PER SERVING):

- **Calories:** 180
- **Protein:** 4g
- **Carbohydrates:** 20g
- **Fat:** 10g
- **Fiber:** 6g
- **Sodium:** 300mg

Enjoy your healthy and flavorful Mediterranean Vegetable Casserole!

Sweet Potato and Black Bean Enchiladas

Prep Time: **10 mins** | Cooking Time: **25 mins**
Yield: **4 portions**

INGREDIENTS:

- 2 sweet potatoes, diced
- 1 can black beans, drained
- 1 onion, chopped
- 2 cloves garlic, minced
- 1 cup enchilada sauce
- 8 corn tortillas
- 2 tbsp olive oil
- 1 tsp cumin
- Salt and pepper to taste
- **Optional:** cilantro, avocado

INSTRUCTIONS:

1. **Cook Vegetables:**
   - Sauté sweet potatoes, onion, and garlic in olive oil until tender. Add beans, cumin, salt, and pepper.
2. **Assemble Enchiladas:**
   - Fill tortillas with mixture, roll up, and place in a baking dish.
3. **Add Sauce:**
   - Pour enchilada sauce over tortillas.
4. **Bake:**
   - Bake at 375°F for 20 minutes.
5. **Serve:**
   - Garnish with cilantro and avocado if desired.

NUTRITIONAL INFORMATION (PER SERVING):

- **Calories:** 350
- **Protein:** 10g
- **Carbohydrates:** 60g
- **Fat:** 8g
- **Fiber:** 12g
- **Sodium:** 500mg

Enjoy your healthy and flavorful Sweet Potato and Black Bean Enchiladas!

Grilled Vegetable Skewers

Prep Time: **10 mins** | Cooking Time: **10 mins**
Yield: **4 portions**

INGREDIENTS:

- 1 zucchini, sliced
- 1 bell pepper, chopped
- 1 red onion, chopped
- 8 cherry tomatoes
- 2 tbsp olive oil
- 1 tsp oregano
- Salt and pepper to taste

INSTRUCTIONS:

1. **Prepare Vegetables:**
   - Toss vegetables with olive oil, oregano, salt, and pepper.
2. **Assemble Skewers:**
   - Thread vegetables onto skewers.
3. **Grill:**
   - Grill for 8-10 minutes, turning occasionally.
4. **Serve:**
   - Serve immediately.

NUTRITIONAL INFORMATION (PER SERVING):

- **Calories:** 100
- **Protein:** 2g
- **Carbohydrates:** 10g
- **Fat:** 7g
- **Fiber:** 3g
- **Sodium:** 150mg

Enjoy your healthy and flavorful Grilled Vegetable Skewers!

Eggplant and Tomato Bake

Prep Time: **10 mins** | Cooking Time: **30 mins**
Yield: **4 portions**

INGREDIENTS:

- 1 eggplant, sliced
- 2 tomatoes, sliced
- 1/2 cup mozzarella, shredded
- 2 tbsp olive oil
- 1 tsp oregano
- Salt and pepper to taste

INSTRUCTIONS:

1. **Prepare Eggplant:**
   - Brush eggplant slices with olive oil, season with salt and pepper. Roast at 375°F for 15 minutes.
2. **Assemble Bake:**
   - Layer eggplant and tomato slices in a baking dish. Top with mozzarella and oregano.
3. **Bake:**
   - Bake at 375°F for 15 minutes until cheese is melted.
4. **Serve:**
   - Serve immediately.

NUTRITIONAL INFORMATION (PER SERVING):

- **Calories:** 150
- **Protein:** 5g
- **Carbohydrates:** 10g
- **Fat:** 10g
- **Fiber:** 4g
- **Sodium:** 200mg

Enjoy your healthy and flavorful Eggplant and Tomato Bake!

Chickpea and Vegetable Tagine

Prep Time: **10 mins** | Cooking Time: **30 mins**
Yield: **4 portions**

INGREDIENTS:

- 1 can chickpeas, drained
- 1 zucchini, diced
- 1 bell pepper, chopped
- 1 carrot, sliced
- 1 onion, chopped
- 2 cloves garlic, minced
- 1 cup vegetable broth
- 1 can diced tomatoes
- 1 tsp cumin
- 1 tsp coriander
- 2 tbsp olive oil
- Salt and pepper to taste

INSTRUCTIONS:

1. **Sauté Vegetables:**
   Sauté onion, garlic, carrot, and bell pepper in olive oil until soft.
2. **Add Ingredients:**
   Add zucchini, chickpeas, tomatoes, broth, cumin, coriander, salt, and pepper. Simmer for 20 minutes.
3. **Serve:**
   Serve immediately.

NUTRITIONAL INFORMATION (PER SERVING):

- **Calories:** 250
- **Protein:** 7g
- **Carbohydrates:** 35g
- **Fat:** 10g
- **Fiber:** 8g
- **Sodium:** 300mg

Enjoy your healthy and flavorful Chickpea and Vegetable Tagine!

Greek Style Stuffed Zucchini

Prep Time: **10 mins** | Cooking Time: **20 mins**
Yield: **4 portions**

INGREDIENTS:

- 4 zucchinis, halved and scooped
- 1 cup cooked quinoa
- 1/2 cup feta cheese, crumbled
- 1/4 cup cherry tomatoes, diced
- 2 tbsp olive oil
- 1 tsp oregano
- Salt and pepper to taste

INSTRUCTIONS:

1. **Prepare Zucchini:**
   Brush zucchini halves with olive oil, season with salt and pepper. Roast at 375°F for 10 minutes.
2. **Mix Filling:**
   Combine quinoa, feta, tomatoes, oregano, salt, and pepper.
3. **Stuff Zucchini:**
   Fill zucchini halves with the quinoa mixture.
4. **Bake:**
   Bake at 375°F for another 10 minutes.
5. **Serve:**
   Serve immediately.

NUTRITIONAL INFORMATION (PER SERVING):

- **Calories:** 200
- **Protein:** 7g
- **Carbohydrates:** 15g
- **Fat:** 12g
- **Fiber:** 4g
- **Sodium:** 250mg

Enjoy your healthy and flavorful Greek Style Stuffed Zucchini!

Tofu and Vegetable Stir-Fry

Prep Time: **10 mins** | Cooking Time: **15 mins**
Yield: **4 portions**

INGREDIENTS:

- 1 block tofu, cubed
- 1 zucchini, sliced
- 1 bell pepper, chopped
- 1 carrot, sliced
- 1 onion, chopped
- 2 cloves garlic, minced
- 2 tbsp olive oil
- 2 tbsp soy sauce
- 1 tsp oregano
- Salt and pepper to taste

INSTRUCTIONS:

1. **Sauté Tofu:**
   - Sauté tofu in olive oil until golden. Remove from skillet.
2. **Cook Vegetables:**
   - Sauté onion, garlic, carrot, and bell pepper until soft. Add zucchini, cook for 3 minutes.
3. **Combine:**
   - Return tofu to skillet. Add soy sauce, oregano, salt, and pepper. Cook for 2 minutes.
4. **Serve:**
   - Serve immediately.

NUTRITIONAL INFORMATION (PER SERVING):

- **Calories:** 250
- **Protein:** 10g
- **Carbohydrates:** 15g
- **Fat:** 16g
- **Fiber:** 4g
- **Sodium:** 300mg

Enjoy your healthy and flavorful Tofu and Vegetable Stir-Fry!

Roasted Garlic and Herb Cauliflower Steaks

Prep Time: **10 mins** | Cooking Time: **25 mins**
Yield: **4 portions**

INGREDIENTS:

- 1 large cauliflower, sliced into steaks
- 3 tbsp olive oil
- 3 cloves garlic, minced
- 1 tsp thyme
- 1 tsp rosemary
- Salt and pepper to taste

INSTRUCTIONS:

1. **Prepare Cauliflower:**
   - Brush cauliflower steaks with olive oil, garlic, thyme, rosemary, salt, and pepper.
2. **Roast:**
   - Roast at 400°F for 25 minutes, turning halfway.
3. **Serve:**
   - Serve immediately.

NUTRITIONAL INFORMATION (PER SERVING):

- **Calories:** 150
- **Protein:** 3g
- **Carbohydrates:** 10g
- **Fat:** 11g
- **Fiber:** 4g
- **Sodium:** 200mg

Enjoy your healthy and flavorful Roasted Garlic and Herb Cauliflower Steaks!

CHAPTER 8. SNACKS AND APPETIZERS

Hummus with Pita Chips

Prep Time: **10 mins** | Cooking Time: **10 mins**
Yield: **4 portions**

INGREDIENTS:

- 1 can chickpeas, drained
- 2 tbsp tahini
- 2 tbsp olive oil
- 1 lemon, juiced
- 2 cloves garlic
- Salt to taste
- 4 pita breads, cut into chips
- **Optional:** paprika, cumin

INSTRUCTIONS:

1. **Make Hummus:**
   - Blend chickpeas, tahini, olive oil, lemon juice, garlic, and salt until smooth.
2. **Bake Pita Chips:**
   - Brush pita chips with olive oil, bake at 375°F for 10 minutes.
3. **Serve:**
   - Serve hummus with pita chips.

NUTRITIONAL INFORMATION (PER SERVING):

- **Calories:** 250
- **Protein:** 7g
- **Carbohydrates:** 30g
- **Fat:** 10g
- **Fiber:** 5g
- **Sodium:** 300mg

Enjoy your healthy and flavorful Hummus with Pita Chips!

Spanakopita Triangles

Prep Time: **15 mins** | Cooking Time: **20 mins**
Yield: **4 portions**

INGREDIENTS:

- 1 lb spinach, chopped
- 1 cup feta cheese, crumbled
- 1 onion, chopped
- 2 cloves garlic, minced
- 2 tbsp olive oil
- 1 egg, beaten
- 1 tsp dill
- Salt and pepper to taste
- 8 sheets phyllo dough
- Additional olive oil for brushing

INSTRUCTIONS:

1. **Prepare Filling:**
   - Sauté onion and garlic in olive oil until soft. Add spinach, cook until wilted. Mix in feta, egg, dill, salt, and pepper.
2. **Assemble Triangles:**
   - Cut phyllo sheets into strips. Place filling on one end, fold into triangles. Brush with olive oil.
3. **Bake:**
   - Bake at 375°F for 20 minutes.
4. **Serve:**
   - Serve immediately.

NUTRITIONAL INFORMATION (PER SERVING):

- **Calories:** 300
- **Protein:** 10g
- **Carbohydrates:** 25g
- **Fat:** 18g
- **Fiber:** 3g
- **Sodium:** 400mg

Enjoy your healthy and flavorful Spanakopita Triangles!

Marinated Olives

Prep Time: **10 mins** | Cooking Time: **None**
Yield: **4 portions**

INGREDIENTS:

- 2 cups mixed olives
- 2 tbsp olive oil
- 2 cloves garlic, minced
- 1 tsp rosemary
- 1 tsp thyme
- 1 lemon, zested
- Salt and pepper to taste

INSTRUCTIONS:

1. **Combine Ingredients:**
   - Mix olives, olive oil, garlic, rosemary, thyme, lemon zest, salt, and pepper.
2. **Marinate:**
   - Let sit for at least 1 hour before serving.
3. **Serve:**
   - Serve at room temperature.

NUTRITIONAL INFORMATION (PER SERVING):

- **Calories:** 150
- **Protein:** 1g
- **Carbohydrates:** 3g
- **Fat:** 15g
- **Fiber:** 2g
- **Sodium:** 400mg

Enjoy your healthy and flavorful Marinated Olives!

Falafel with Tzatziki

Prep Time: **15 mins** | Cooking Time: **20 mins**
Yield: **4 portions**

INGREDIENTS:

Falafel:
- 1 can chickpeas, drained
- 1/4 cup parsley, chopped
- 2 cloves garlic, minced
- 1 tsp cumin
- 1 tsp coriander
- 2 tbsp flour
- Salt and pepper to taste
- 2 tbsp olive oil

Tzatziki:
- 1 cup Greek yogurt
- 1 cucumber, grated
- 1 clove garlic, minced
- 1 tbsp lemon juice
- 1 tbsp dill, chopped
- Salt to taste

INSTRUCTIONS:

1. **Prepare Falafel:**
   - Blend chickpeas, parsley, garlic, cumin, coriander, flour, salt, and pepper. Form into patties.
2. **Cook Falafel:**
   - Sauté in olive oil over medium heat, 3-4 minutes per side.
3. **Prepare Tzatziki:**
   - Mix yogurt, cucumber, garlic, lemon juice, dill, and salt.
4. **Serve:**
   - Serve falafel with tzatziki.

NUTRITIONAL INFORMATION (PER SERVING):

- **Calories:** 300
- **Protein:** 10g
- **Carbohydrates:** 30g
- **Fat:** 15g
- **Fiber:** 8g
- **Sodium:** 400mg

Enjoy your healthy and flavorful Falafel with Tzatziki!

Feta Stuffed Dates

Prep Time: **10 mins** | Cooking Time: **None**
Yield: **4 portions**

INGREDIENTS:

- 16 dates, pitted
- 1/2 cup feta cheese, crumbled
- 1 tbsp olive oil
- **Optional:** chopped nuts or herbs

INSTRUCTIONS:

1. **Stuff Dates:**
   Fill each date with feta cheese.
2. **Drizzle:**
   Drizzle with olive oil.
3. **Garnish:**
   Optional: top with chopped nuts or herbs.
4. **Serve:**
   Serve immediately.

NUTRITIONAL INFORMATION (PER SERVING):

- **Calories:** 150
- **Protein:** 4g
- **Carbohydrates:** 25g
- **Fat:** 5g
- **Fiber:** 3g
- **Sodium:** 150mg

Enjoy your healthy and flavorful Feta Stuffed Dates!

Mediterranean Bruschetta

Prep Time: **10 mins** | Cooking Time: **5 mins**
Yield: **4 portions**

INGREDIENTS:

- 8 slices whole-grain baguette
- 2 cups cherry tomatoes, diced
- 1/4 cup feta cheese, crumbled
- 2 tbsp olive oil
- 1 clove garlic, minced
- 1 tbsp basil, chopped
- Salt and pepper to taste

INSTRUCTIONS:

1. **Toast Bread:**
   Toast baguette slices in a skillet or oven until golden.
2. **Prepare Topping:**
   Mix tomatoes, feta, olive oil, garlic, basil, salt, and pepper.
3. **Assemble Bruschetta:**
   Spoon tomato mixture onto toasted bread.
4. **Serve:**
   Serve immediately.

NUTRITIONAL INFORMATION (PER SERVING):

- **Calories:** 150
- **Protein:** 4g
- **Carbohydrates:** 20g
- **Fat:** 7g
- **Fiber:** 3g
- **Sodium:** 200mg

Enjoy your healthy and flavorful Mediterranean Bruschetta!

Lemon and Herb Marinated Feta

Prep Time: **5 mins** | Marinate Time: **1 hour**
Yield: **4 portions**

INGREDIENTS:

- 1 cup feta cheese, cubed
- 2 tbsp olive oil
- 1 lemon, zested and juiced
- 1 tbsp fresh herbs (parsley, oregano), chopped
- Salt and pepper to taste

INSTRUCTIONS:

1. **Marinate Feta:**
   - Mix olive oil, lemon zest, lemon juice, herbs, salt, and pepper. Toss with feta cubes.
2. **Chill:**
   - Marinate in the refrigerator for 1 hour.
3. **Serve:**
   - Serve chilled.

NUTRITIONAL INFORMATION (PER SERVING):

- **Calories:** 150
- **Protein:** 5g
- **Carbohydrates:** 2g
- **Fat:** 13g
- **Fiber:** 0g
- **Sodium:** 350mg

Enjoy your healthy and flavorful Lemon and Herb Marinated Feta!

Zucchini Fritters

Prep Time: **10 mins** | Cooking Time: **10 mins**
Yield: **4 portions**

INGREDIENTS:

- 2 zucchinis, grated
- 1/4 cup flour
- 1/4 cup feta cheese, crumbled
- 1 egg, beaten
- 2 cloves garlic, minced
- 2 tbsp olive oil
- 1 tbsp fresh herbs (dill, parsley), chopped
- Salt and pepper to taste

INSTRUCTIONS:

1. **Prepare Mixture:**
   - Combine zucchini, flour, feta, egg, garlic, herbs, salt, and pepper.
2. **Form Fritters:**
   - Shape mixture into small patties.
3. **Cook:**
   - Heat olive oil in a skillet. Fry fritters until golden, about 3-4 minutes per side.
4. **Serve:**
   - Serve immediately.

NUTRITIONAL INFORMATION (PER SERVING):

- **Calories:** 150
- **Protein:** 5g
- **Carbohydrates:** 10g
- **Fat:** 10g
- **Fiber:** 2g
- **Sodium:** 250mg

Enjoy your healthy and flavorful Zucchini Fritters!

Garlic Shrimp Skewers

Prep Time: **10 mins** | Cooking Time: **10 mins**
Yield: **4 portions**

INGREDIENTS:

- 1 lb shrimp, peeled and deveined
- 3 cloves garlic, minced
- 2 tbsp olive oil
- 1 lemon, juiced
- 1 tbsp fresh parsley, chopped
- Salt and pepper to taste

INSTRUCTIONS:

1. **Marinate Shrimp:**
   - Toss shrimp with garlic, olive oil, lemon juice, salt, and pepper. Marinate for 10 minutes.
2. **Assemble Skewers:**
   - Thread shrimp onto skewers.
3. **Grill:**
   - Grill over medium heat for 2-3 minutes per side until pink and opaque.
4. **Serve:**
   - Sprinkle with parsley and serve immediately.

NUTRITIONAL INFORMATION (PER SERVING):

- **Calories:** 200
- **Protein:** 20g
- **Carbohydrates:** 2g
- **Fat:** 12g
- **Fiber:** 0g
- **Sodium:** 300mg

Enjoy your healthy and flavorful Garlic Shrimp Skewers!

Stuffed Grape Leaves

Prep Time: **15 mins** | Cooking Time: **30 mins**
Yield: **4 portions**

INGREDIENTS:

- 1 jar grape leaves, drained
- 1 cup cooked rice
- 1/4 cup pine nuts
- 1/4 cup parsley, chopped
- 2 tbsp lemon juice
- 2 tbsp olive oil
- 1 onion, chopped
- Salt and pepper to taste

INSTRUCTIONS:

1. **Prepare Filling:**
   - Sauté onion in olive oil until soft. Mix with rice, pine nuts, parsley, salt, and pepper.
2. **Stuff Leaves:**
   - Place a spoonful of filling on each leaf, roll tightly.
3. **Cook:**
   - Arrange in a pot, drizzle with lemon juice, add water to cover. Simmer for 30 minutes.
4. **Serve:**
   - Serve warm or cold.

NUTRITIONAL INFORMATION (PER SERVING):

- **Calories:** 150
- **Protein:** 3g
- **Carbohydrates:** 18g
- **Fat:** 7g
- **Fiber:** 2g
- **Sodium:** 300mg

Enjoy your healthy and flavorful Stuffed Grape Leaves!

Sun-Dried Tomato Tapenade

Prep Time: **10 mins** | Cooking Time: **None**
Yield: **4 portions**

INGREDIENTS:

- 1 cup sun-dried tomatoes
- 1/2 cup olives, pitted
- 2 tbsp capers
- 2 cloves garlic
- 1/4 cup olive oil
- Salt and pepper to taste

INSTRUCTIONS:

1. **Blend:**
   - Combine all ingredients in a food processor. Blend until smooth.
2. **Serve:**
   - Serve immediately or chill.

NUTRITIONAL INFORMATION (PER SERVING):

- **Calories:** 180
- **Protein:** 2g
- **Carbohydrates:** 6g
- **Fat:** 16g
- **Fiber:** 2g
- **Sodium:** 350mg

Enjoy your healthy and flavorful Sun-Dried Tomato Tapenade!

Smoked Salmon Crostini

Prep Time: **10 mins** | Cooking Time: **5 mins**
Yield: **4 portions**

INGREDIENTS:

- 8 slices baguette
- 4 oz smoked salmon
- 1/4 cup cream cheese
- 1 tbsp capers
- 1 tbsp dill, chopped
- 1 tbsp lemon juice
- Salt and pepper to taste

INSTRUCTIONS:

1. **Toast Baguette:**
   - Toast baguette slices until golden.
2. **Assemble Crostini:**
   - Spread cream cheese on each slice, top with smoked salmon, capers, dill, and a squeeze of lemon juice. Season with salt and pepper.
3. **Serve:**
   - Serve immediately.

NUTRITIONAL INFORMATION (PER SERVING):

- **Calories:** 200
- **Protein:** 10g
- **Carbohydrates:** 15g
- **Fat:** 12g
- **Fiber:** 1g
- **Sodium:** 400mg

Enjoy your healthy and flavorful Smoked Salmon Crostini!

Greek Yogurt Dip with Fresh Veggies

Prep Time: **10 mins** | Cooking Time: **None**
Yield: **4 portions**

INGREDIENTS:

- 1 cup Greek yogurt
- 1 tbsp lemon juice
- 1 tbsp olive oil
- 1 garlic clove, minced
- 1 tbsp dill, chopped
- Salt and pepper to taste
- Fresh veggies (carrots, cucumbers, bell peppers), sliced

INSTRUCTIONS:

1. **Prepare Dip:**
   - Mix yogurt, lemon juice, olive oil, garlic, dill, salt, and pepper.
2. **Serve:**
   - Serve dip with fresh veggies.

NUTRITIONAL INFORMATION (PER SERVING):

- **Calories:** 120
- **Protein:** 8g
- **Carbohydrates:** 10g
- **Fat:** 6g
- **Fiber:** 2g
- **Sodium:** 150mg

Enjoy your healthy and flavorful Greek Yogurt Dip with Fresh Veggies!

Roasted Eggplant Dip

Prep Time: **10 mins** | Cooking Time: **30 mins**
Yield: **4 portions**

INGREDIENTS:

- 1 large eggplant
- 2 tbsp olive oil
- 2 cloves garlic, minced
- 1 tbsp lemon juice
- 1 tbsp tahini
- Salt and pepper to taste

INSTRUCTIONS:

1. **Roast Eggplant:**
   - Roast eggplant at 400°F for 30 minutes until soft.
2. **Blend:**
   - Scoop out eggplant flesh and blend with olive oil, garlic, lemon juice, tahini, salt, and pepper until smooth.
3. **Serve:**
   - Serve with pita or veggies.

NUTRITIONAL INFORMATION (PER SERVING):

- **Calories:** 100
- **Protein:** 2g
- **Carbohydrates:** 10g
- **Fat:** 7g
- **Fiber:** 4g
- **Sodium:** 150mg

Enjoy your healthy and flavorful Roasted Eggplant Dip!

Cheese and Olive Platter

Prep Time: **10 mins** | Cooking Time: **None**
Yield: **4 portions**

INGREDIENTS:

- 1 cup assorted olives
- 1 cup feta cheese, cubed
- 1 cup cherry tomatoes
- 1/4 cup olive oil
- 1 tsp oregano
- Salt and pepper to taste

INSTRUCTIONS:

1. **Assemble Platter:**
   - Arrange olives, feta, and tomatoes on a platter.
2. **Season:**
   - Drizzle with olive oil, sprinkle with oregano, salt, and pepper.
3. **Serve:**
   - Serve immediately.

NUTRITIONAL INFORMATION (PER SERVING):

- **Calories:** 250
- **Protein:** 8g
- **Carbohydrates:** 5g
- **Fat:** 22g
- **Fiber:** 2g
- **Sodium:** 500mg

Enjoy your healthy and flavorful Cheese and Olive Platter!

Pita Chips with Lemon Garlic Hummus

Prep Time: **10 mins** | Cooking Time: **10 mins**
Yield: **4 portions**

INGREDIENTS:

Pita Chips:
- 4 pita breads, cut into wedges
- 2 tbsp olive oil
- Salt to taste

Lemon Garlic Hummus:
- 1 can chickpeas, drained
- 2 tbsp tahini
- 2 tbsp olive oil
- 1 lemon, juiced
- 2 cloves garlic
- Salt and pepper to taste

INSTRUCTIONS:

1. **Make Pita Chips:**
   - Brush pita wedges with olive oil, sprinkle with salt. Bake at 375°F for 10 minutes.
2. **Prepare Hummus:**
   - Blend chickpeas, tahini, olive oil, lemon juice, garlic, salt, and pepper until smooth.
3. **Serve:**
   - Serve pita chips with hummus.

NUTRITIONAL INFORMATION (PER SERVING):

- **Calories:** 300
- **Protein:** 8g
- **Carbohydrates:** 40g
- **Fat:** 12g
- **Fiber:** 8g
- **Sodium:** 400mg

Enjoy your healthy and flavorful Pita Chips with Lemon Garlic Hummus!

CHAPTER 9. PASTA

Spaghetti Aglio e Olio

Prep Time: **5 mins** | Cooking Time: **15 mins**
Yield: **4 portions**

INGREDIENTS:

- 12 oz spaghetti
- 1/4 cup olive oil
- 4 cloves garlic, thinly sliced
- 1/4 tsp red pepper flakes
- Salt to taste
- 1/4 cup parsley, chopped
- **Optional:** grated Parmesan cheese

INSTRUCTIONS:

1. **Cook Spaghetti:**
   ◇ Boil spaghetti until al dente. Drain and set aside.
2. **Sauté Garlic:**
   ◇ Heat olive oil in a skillet, sauté garlic and red pepper flakes until golden.
3. **Combine:**
   ◇ Toss spaghetti in the skillet with garlic oil. Add salt and parsley.
4. **Serve:**
   ◇ Serve immediately, topped with Parmesan if desired.

NUTRITIONAL INFORMATION (PER SERVING):

- **Calories:** 400
- **Protein:** 10g
- **Carbohydrates:** 60g
- **Fat:** 15g
- **Fiber:** 3g
- **Sodium:** 150mg

Enjoy your healthy and flavorful Spaghetti Aglio e Olio!

Lemon and Artichoke Penne

Prep Time: **5 mins** | Cooking Time: **15 mins**
Yield: **4 portions**

INGREDIENTS:

- 12 oz penne pasta
- 1 can artichoke hearts, drained and quartered
- 2 tbsp olive oil
- 2 cloves garlic, minced
- 1 lemon, zested and juiced
- 1/4 cup Parmesan cheese, grated
- Salt and pepper to taste
- 1/4 cup parsley, chopped

INSTRUCTIONS:

1. **Cook Penne:**
   ◇ Boil penne until al dente. Drain and set aside.
2. **Sauté Garlic:**
   ◇ Heat olive oil in a skillet, sauté garlic until fragrant.
3. **Combine:**
   ◇ Add artichokes, lemon zest, and juice to the skillet. Toss with penne. Add salt, pepper, and Parmesan.
4. **Serve:**
   ◇ Garnish with parsley and serve immediately.

NUTRITIONAL INFORMATION (PER SERVING):

- **Calories:** 350
- **Protein:** 12g
- **Carbohydrates:** 55g
- **Fat:** 10g
- **Fiber:** 5g
- **Sodium:** 200mg

Enjoy your healthy and flavorful Lemon and Artichoke Penne!

Shrimp and Feta Linguine

Prep Time: **10 mins** | Cooking Time: **15 mins**
Yield: **4 portions**

INGREDIENTS:

- 12 oz linguine
- 1 lb shrimp, peeled and deveined
- 2 tbsp olive oil
- 3 cloves garlic, minced
- 1 cup cherry tomatoes, halved
- 1/2 cup feta cheese, crumbled
- 1/4 cup parsley, chopped
- Salt and pepper to taste

INSTRUCTIONS:

1. **Cook Linguine:**
   - Boil linguine until al dente. Drain and set aside.
2. **Sauté Shrimp:**
   - Heat olive oil in a skillet, sauté garlic until fragrant. Add shrimp, cook until pink.
3. **Combine:**
   - Add tomatoes and cooked linguine to the skillet. Toss with feta, parsley, salt, and pepper.
4. **Serve:**
   - Serve immediately.

NUTRITIONAL INFORMATION (PER SERVING):

- **Calories:** 400
- **Protein:** 25g
- **Carbohydrates:** 45g
- **Fat:** 15g
- **Fiber:** 3g
- **Sodium:** 350mg

Enjoy your healthy and flavorful Shrimp and Feta Linguine!

Greek Style Stuffed Shells

Prep Time: **10 mins** | Cooking Time: **25 mins**
Yield: **4 portions**

INGREDIENTS:

- 12 jumbo pasta shells
- 1 cup ricotta cheese
- 1/2 cup feta cheese, crumbled
- 1 cup spinach, chopped
- 1 egg, beaten
- 2 cloves garlic, minced
- 2 cups marinara sauce
- Salt and pepper to taste

INSTRUCTIONS:

1. **Cook Shells:**
   - Boil shells until al dente. Drain and set aside.
2. **Prepare Filling:**
   - Mix ricotta, feta, spinach, egg, garlic, salt, and pepper.
3. **Stuff Shells:**
   - Fill shells with the cheese mixture. Place in a baking dish with marinara sauce.
4. **Bake:**
   - Bake at 375°F for 20 minutes.
5. **Serve:**
   - Serve immediately.

NUTRITIONAL INFORMATION (PER SERVING):

- **Calories:** 300
- **Protein:** 15g
- **Carbohydrates:** 30g
- **Fat:** 15g
- **Fiber:** 3g
- **Sodium:** 400mg

Enjoy your healthy and flavorful Greek Style Stuffed Shells!

Pasta with Anchovy Sauce

Prep Time: **5 mins** | Cooking Time: **10 mins**
Yield: **4 portions**

INGREDIENTS:

- 12 oz pasta
- 6 anchovy fillets, chopped
- 2 cloves garlic, minced
- 1/4 cup olive oil
- 1/4 tsp red pepper flakes
- 1/4 cup parsley, chopped
- Salt and pepper to taste

INSTRUCTIONS:

1. **Cook Pasta:**
   Boil pasta until al dente. Drain and set aside.
2. **Prepare Sauce:**
   Heat olive oil in a skillet. Sauté garlic and red pepper flakes until fragrant. Add anchovies and cook until dissolved.
3. **Combine:**
   Toss pasta with sauce and parsley. Season with salt and pepper.
4. **Serve:**
   Serve immediately.

NUTRITIONAL INFORMATION (PER SERVING):

- **Calories:** 400
- **Protein:** 12g
- **Carbohydrates:** 60g
- **Fat:** 15g
- **Fiber:** 3g
- **Sodium:** 350mg

Enjoy your healthy and flavorful Pasta with Anchovy Sauce!

Lemon and Garlic Shrimp Pasta

Prep Time: **5 mins** | Cooking Time: **10 mins**
Yield: **4 portions**

INGREDIENTS:

- 12 oz pasta
- 1 lb shrimp, peeled and deveined
- 3 cloves garlic, minced
- 1/4 cup olive oil
- 1 lemon, zested and juiced
- 1/4 cup parsley, chopped
- Salt and pepper to taste

INSTRUCTIONS:

1. **Cook Pasta:**
   Boil pasta until al dente. Drain and set aside.
2. **Sauté Shrimp:**
   Heat olive oil in a skillet. Sauté garlic until fragrant. Add shrimp and cook until pink.
3. **Combine:**
   Toss pasta with shrimp, lemon zest, lemon juice, parsley, salt, and pepper.
4. **Serve:**
   Serve immediately.

NUTRITIONAL INFORMATION (PER SERVING):

- **Calories:** 400
- **Protein:** 25g
- **Carbohydrates:** 50g
- **Fat:** 12g
- **Fiber:** 3g
- **Sodium:** 300mg

Enjoy your healthy and flavorful Lemon and Garlic Shrimp Pasta!

Fettuccine with Roasted Tomatoes

Prep Time: **5 mins** | Cooking Time: **20 mins**
Yield: **4 portions**

INGREDIENTS:

- 12 oz fettuccine
- 2 cups cherry tomatoes, halved
- 3 cloves garlic, minced
- 1/4 cup olive oil
- 1/4 cup Parmesan cheese, grated
- 1/4 cup basil, chopped
- Salt and pepper to taste

INSTRUCTIONS:

1. **Roast Tomatoes:**
   Toss tomatoes with olive oil, garlic, salt, and pepper. Roast at 400°F for 15 minutes.
2. **Cook Fettuccine:**
   Boil fettuccine until al dente. Drain and set aside.
3. **Combine:**
   Toss fettuccine with roasted tomatoes, Parmesan, and basil.
4. **Serve:**
   Serve immediately.

NUTRITIONAL INFORMATION (PER SERVING):

- **Calories:** 350
- **Protein:** 12g
- **Carbohydrates:** 55g
- **Fat:** 10g
- **Fiber:** 4g
- **Sodium:** 200mg

Enjoy your healthy and flavorful Fettuccine with Roasted Tomatoes!

Penne Arrabbiata with Olives

Prep Time: **5 mins** | Cooking Time: **15 mins**
Yield: **4 portions**

INGREDIENTS:

- 12 oz penne pasta
- 2 cups tomato sauce
- 1/4 cup olives, sliced
- 3 cloves garlic, minced
- 1 tsp red pepper flakes
- 2 tbsp olive oil
- Salt and pepper to taste
- 1/4 cup parsley, chopped

INSTRUCTIONS:

1. **Cook Penne:**
   Boil penne until al dente. Drain and set aside.
2. **Prepare Sauce:**
   Sauté garlic and red pepper flakes in olive oil until fragrant. Add tomato sauce and olives. Simmer for 10 minutes.
3. **Combine:**
   Toss penne with sauce. Season with salt, pepper, and parsley.
4. **Serve:**
   Serve immediately.

NUTRITIONAL INFORMATION (PER SERVING):

- **Calories:** 350
- **Protein:** 10g
- **Carbohydrates:** 60g
- **Fat:** 10g
- **Fiber:** 5g
- **Sodium:** 300mg

Enjoy your healthy and flavorful Penne Arrabbiata with Olives!

Tomato and Basil Penne

Prep Time: **5 mins** | Cooking Time: **15 mins**
Yield: **4 portions**

INGREDIENTS:

- 12 oz penne pasta
- 2 cups cherry tomatoes, halved
- 3 cloves garlic, minced
- 1/4 cup olive oil
- 1/4 cup fresh basil, chopped
- Salt and pepper to taste
- 1/4 cup Parmesan cheese, grated (optional)

INSTRUCTIONS:

1. **Cook Penne:**
   Boil penne until al dente. Drain and set aside.
2. **Prepare Sauce:**
   Sauté garlic in olive oil until fragrant. Add cherry tomatoes, cook until softened.
3. **Combine:**
   Toss penne with tomato mixture, basil, salt, and pepper.
4. **Serve:**
   Serve immediately, topped with Parmesan if desired.

NUTRITIONAL INFORMATION (PER SERVING):

- **Calories:** 350
- **Protein:** 10g
- **Carbohydrates:** 60g
- **Fat:** 10g
- **Fiber:** 4g
- **Sodium:** 150mg

Enjoy your healthy and flavorful Tomato and Basil Penne!

Whole Wheat Spaghetti with Clams

Prep Time: **5 mins** | Cooking Time: **15 mins**
Yield: **4 portions**

INGREDIENTS:

- 12 oz whole wheat spaghetti
- 2 lbs clams, cleaned
- 3 cloves garlic, minced
- 1/4 cup olive oil
- 1/2 cup white wine
- 1/4 cup parsley, chopped
- Salt and pepper to taste
- **Optional:** red pepper flakes

INSTRUCTIONS:

1. **Cook Spaghetti:**
   Boil spaghetti until al dente. Drain and set aside.
2. **Prepare Clams:**
   Sauté garlic in olive oil until fragrant. Add clams and white wine. Cover and cook until clams open, about 5 minutes.
3. **Combine:**
   Toss spaghetti with clams and sauce. Add parsley, salt, and pepper.
4. **Serve:**
   Serve immediately, topped with red pepper flakes if desired.

NUTRITIONAL INFORMATION (PER SERVING):

- **Calories:** 400
- **Protein:** 20g
- **Carbohydrates:** 60g
- **Fat:** 10g
- **Fiber:** 6g
- **Sodium:** 300mg

Enjoy your healthy and flavorful Whole Wheat Spaghetti with Clams!

Pesto and Sun-Dried Tomato Penne

Prep Time: **5 mins** | Cooking Time: **15 mins**
Yield: **4 portions**

INGREDIENTS:

- 12 oz penne pasta
- 1/2 cup pesto
- 1/4 cup sun-dried tomatoes, chopped
- 2 tbsp olive oil
- 1/4 cup Parmesan cheese, grated (optional)
- Salt and pepper to taste

INSTRUCTIONS:

1. **Cook Penne:**
   - Boil penne until al dente. Drain and set aside.
2. **Combine:**
   - Toss penne with pesto, sun-dried tomatoes, olive oil, salt, and pepper.
3. **Serve:**
   - Serve immediately, topped with Parmesan if desired.

NUTRITIONAL INFORMATION (PER SERVING):

- **Calories:** 350
- **Protein:** 10g
- **Carbohydrates:** 50g
- **Fat:** 15g
- **Fiber:** 4g
- **Sodium:** 200mg

Enjoy your healthy and flavorful Pesto and Sun-Dried Tomato Penne!

Ricotta and Spinach Stuffed Manicotti

Prep Time: **10 mins** | Cooking Time: **25 mins**
Yield: **4 portions**

INGREDIENTS:

- 8 manicotti shells
- 1 cup ricotta cheese
- 1 cup spinach, chopped
- 1/2 cup mozzarella, shredded
- 1 egg, beaten
- 2 cups marinara sauce
- Salt and pepper to taste

INSTRUCTIONS:

1. **Cook Manicotti:**
   - Boil manicotti until al dente. Drain and set aside.
2. **Prepare Filling:**
   - Mix ricotta, spinach, mozzarella, egg, salt, and pepper.
3. **Stuff Shells:**
   - Fill manicotti with cheese mixture. Place in a baking dish with marinara sauce.
4. **Bake:**
   - Bake at 375°F for 20 minutes.
5. **Serve:**
   - Serve immediately.

NUTRITIONAL INFORMATION (PER SERVING):

- **Calories:** 350
- **Protein:** 15g
- **Carbohydrates:** 45g
- **Fat:** 15g
- **Fiber:** 5g
- **Sodium:** 300mg

Enjoy your healthy and flavorful Ricotta and Spinach Stuffed Manicotti!

Caprese Pasta with Fresh Basil

Prep Time: **5 mins** | Cooking Time: **15 mins**
Yield: **4 portions**

INGREDIENTS:

- 12 oz pasta
- 2 cups cherry tomatoes, halved
- 1 cup mozzarella balls
- 1/4 cup olive oil
- 1/4 cup fresh basil, chopped
- Salt and pepper to taste

INSTRUCTIONS:

1. **Cook Pasta:**
   Boil pasta until al dente. Drain and set aside.
2. **Combine Ingredients:**
   Toss pasta with tomatoes, mozzarella, olive oil, basil, salt, and pepper.
3. **Serve:**
   Serve immediately.

NUTRITIONAL INFORMATION (PER SERVING):

- **Calories:** 400
- **Protein:** 15g
- **Carbohydrates:** 55g
- **Fat:** 15g
- **Fiber:** 3g
- **Sodium:** 250mg

Enjoy your healthy and flavorful Caprese Pasta with Fresh Basil!

Chickpea Pasta with Garlic and Parsley

Prep Time: **5 mins** | Cooking Time: **15 mins**
Yield: **4 portions**

INGREDIENTS:

- 12 oz chickpea pasta
- 4 cloves garlic, minced
- 1/4 cup olive oil
- 1/4 cup fresh parsley, chopped
- Salt and pepper to taste
- **Optional:** red pepper flakes

INSTRUCTIONS:

1. **Cook Pasta:**
   Boil chickpea pasta until al dente. Drain and set aside.
2. **Sauté Garlic:**
   Sauté garlic in olive oil until fragrant.
3. **Combine:**
   Toss pasta with garlic oil, parsley, salt, pepper, and red pepper flakes if desired.
4. **Serve:**
   Serve immediately.

NUTRITIONAL INFORMATION (PER SERVING):

- **Calories:** 350
- **Protein:** 20g
- **Carbohydrates:** 40g
- **Fat:** 12g
- **Fiber:** 8g
- **Sodium:** 200mg

Enjoy your healthy and flavorful Chickpea Pasta with Garlic and Parsley!

Zucchini Noodles with Marinara

Prep Time: **10 mins** | Cooking Time: **10 mins**
Yield: **4 portions**

INGREDIENTS:

- 4 zucchinis, spiralized
- 2 cups marinara sauce
- 2 tbsp olive oil
- 2 cloves garlic, minced
- Salt and pepper to taste
- **Optional:** Parmesan cheese

INSTRUCTIONS:

1. **Sauté Garlic:**
   - Sauté garlic in olive oil until fragrant.
2. **Cook Zoodles:**
   - Add zucchini noodles, cook for 2-3 minutes until tender.
3. **Add Sauce:**
   - Stir in marinara sauce, cook until heated through. Season with salt and pepper.
4. **Serve:**
   - Serve immediately, topped with Parmesan if desired.

NUTRITIONAL INFORMATION (PER SERVING):

- **Calories:** 150
- **Protein:** 3g
- **Carbohydrates:** 15g
- **Fat:** 8g
- **Fiber:** 4g
- **Sodium:** 300mg

Enjoy your healthy and flavorful Zucchini Noodles with Marinara!

Pappardelle with Mushroom Ragu

Prep Time: **5 mins** | Cooking Time: **20 mins**
Yield: **4 portions**

INGREDIENTS:

- 12 oz pappardelle pasta
- 2 cups mushrooms, sliced
- 1 onion, chopped
- 3 cloves garlic, minced
- 1/4 cup olive oil
- 1 cup vegetable broth
- 1/4 cup Parmesan cheese, grated
- Salt and pepper to taste
- 1/4 cup parsley, chopped

INSTRUCTIONS:

1. **Cook Pappardelle:**
   - Boil pappardelle until al dente. Drain and set aside.
2. **Prepare Ragu:**
   - Sauté onion and garlic in olive oil until soft. Add mushrooms, cook until tender. Add broth, simmer for 10 minutes.
3. **Combine:**
   - Toss pasta with mushroom ragu. Season with salt, pepper, and parsley.
4. **Serve:**
   - Serve immediately, topped with Parmesan.

NUTRITIONAL INFORMATION (PER SERVING):

- **Calories:** 400
- **Protein:** 12g
- **Carbohydrates:** 55g
- **Fat:** 15g
- **Fiber:** 4g
- **Sodium:** 300mg

Enjoy your healthy and flavorful Pappardelle with Mushroom Ragu!

CHAPTER 10. PIZZAZ, WRAPS, AND SANDWICHES

Mediterranean Veggie Pizza

Prep Time: **10 mins** | Cooking Time: **15 mins**
Yield: **4 portions**

INGREDIENTS:

- 1 whole wheat pizza crust
- 1/2 cup marinara sauce
- 1 cup mozzarella cheese, shredded
- 1/2 cup cherry tomatoes, halved
- 1/2 cup bell peppers, sliced
- 1/4 cup olives, sliced
- 1/4 cup red onion, sliced
- 2 tbsp olive oil
- 1 tsp oregano
- Salt and pepper to taste

INSTRUCTIONS:

1. **Preheat Oven:**
   - Preheat oven to 425°F.
2. **Assemble Pizza:**
   - Spread marinara sauce on pizza crust. Top with cheese, tomatoes, peppers, olives, and onion. Drizzle with olive oil and sprinkle with oregano, salt, and pepper.
3. **Bake:**
   - Bake for 15 minutes until crust is golden and cheese is melted.
4. **Serve:**
   - Serve immediately.

NUTRITIONAL INFORMATION (PER SERVING):

- **Calories:** 350
- **Protein:** 15g
- **Carbohydrates:** 40g
- **Fat:** 15g
- **Fiber:** 5g
- **Sodium:** 600mg

Enjoy your healthy and flavorful Mediterranean Veggie Pizza!

Greek Gyro Wraps

Prep Time: **10 mins** | Cooking Time: **15 mins**
Yield: **4 portions**

INGREDIENTS:

- 1 lb chicken breast, sliced
- 1 tbsp olive oil
- 1 tsp oregano
- Salt and pepper to taste
- 4 whole wheat pitas
- 1 cup tzatziki sauce
- 1 cup lettuce, shredded
- 1/2 cup cherry tomatoes, halved
- 1/4 cup red onion, sliced

INSTRUCTIONS:

1. **Cook Chicken:**
   - Sauté chicken with olive oil, oregano, salt, and pepper until fully cooked.
2. **Assemble Wraps:**
   - Fill pitas with chicken, tzatziki, lettuce, tomatoes, and onion.
3. **Serve:**
   - Serve immediately.

NUTRITIONAL INFORMATION (PER SERVING):

- **Calories:** 350
- **Protein:** 25g
- **Carbohydrates:** 35g
- **Fat:** 12g
- **Fiber:** 4g
- **Sodium:** 450mg

Enjoy your healthy and flavorful Greek Gyro Wraps!

Hummus and Veggie Wraps

Prep Time: **10 mins** | Cooking Time: **None**
Yield: **4 portions**

INGREDIENTS:

- 4 whole wheat tortillas
- 1 cup hummus
- 1 cup spinach
- 1/2 cup cucumber, sliced
- 1/2 cup bell peppers, sliced
- 1/4 cup red onion, sliced
- 1/4 cup cherry tomatoes, halved
- Salt and pepper to taste

INSTRUCTIONS:

1. **Assemble Wraps:**
    Spread hummus on tortillas. Add spinach, cucumber, bell peppers, onion, and tomatoes. Season with salt and pepper.
2. **Wrap:**
    Roll up tortillas tightly.
3. **Serve:**
    Serve immediately.

NUTRITIONAL INFORMATION (PER SERVING):

- **Calories:** 300
- **Protein:** 8g
- **Carbohydrates:** 40g
- **Fat:** 12g
- **Fiber:** 8g
- **Sodium:** 350mg

Enjoy your healthy and flavorful Hummus and Veggie Wraps!

Caprese Sandwich

Prep Time: **10 mins** | Cooking Time: **None**
Yield: **4 portions**

INGREDIENTS:

- 8 slices whole grain bread
- 2 cups fresh mozzarella, sliced
- 2 tomatoes, sliced
- 1/4 cup fresh basil leaves
- 2 tbsp olive oil
- 1 tbsp balsamic glaze
- Salt and pepper to taste

INSTRUCTIONS:

1. **Assemble Sandwiches:**
    Layer mozzarella, tomatoes, and basil on 4 bread slices. Drizzle with olive oil and balsamic glaze. Season with salt and pepper.
2. **Top:**
    Place remaining bread slices on top.
3. **Serve:**
    Serve immediately.

NUTRITIONAL INFORMATION (PER SERVING):

- **Calories:** 350
- **Protein:** 15g
- **Carbohydrates:** 35g
- **Fat:** 18g
- **Fiber:** 5g
- **Sodium:** 400mg

Enjoy your healthy and flavorful Caprese Sandwich!

Falafel Pita

Prep Time: **10 mins** | Cooking Time: **15 mins**
Yield: **4 portions**

INGREDIENTS:

- 1 can chickpeas, drained
- 1/4 cup parsley, chopped
- 2 cloves garlic, minced
- 1 tsp cumin
- 1 tsp coriander
- 2 tbsp flour
- Salt and pepper to taste
- 2 tbsp olive oil
- 4 whole wheat pitas
- 1 cup lettuce, shredded
- 1/2 cup tomatoes, diced
- 1/2 cup cucumber, sliced
- 1/4 cup tahini sauce

INSTRUCTIONS:

1. **Make Falafel:**
   Blend chickpeas, parsley, garlic, cumin, coriander, flour, salt, and pepper. Form into balls.
2. **Cook Falafel:**
   Sauté falafel in olive oil until golden, about 3-4 minutes per side.
3. **Assemble Pitas:**
   Fill pitas with falafel, lettuce, tomatoes, cucumber, and drizzle with tahini sauce.
4. **Serve:**
   Serve immediately.

NUTRITIONAL INFORMATION (PER SERVING):

- **Calories:** 400
- **Protein:** 12g
- **Carbohydrates:** 50g
- **Fat:** 16g
- **Fiber:** 10g
- **Sodium:** 500mg

Enjoy your healthy and flavorful Falafel Pita!

Grilled Chicken Pesto Panini

Prep Time: **10 mins** | Cooking Time: **15 mins**
Yield: **4 portions**

INGREDIENTS:

- 2 chicken breasts, grilled and sliced
- 8 slices whole grain bread
- 1/2 cup pesto
- 1 cup mozzarella cheese, shredded
- 1 tomato, sliced
- 2 tbsp olive oil
- Salt and pepper to taste

INSTRUCTIONS:

1. **Assemble Paninis:**
   Spread pesto on bread slices. Layer chicken, mozzarella, and tomato. Season with salt and pepper. Top with remaining bread slices.
2. **Grill:**
   Brush panini with olive oil. Grill on skillet or panini press until golden and cheese melts.
3. **Serve:**
   Serve immediately.

NUTRITIONAL INFORMATION (PER SERVING):

- **Calories:** 450
- **Protein:** 25g
- **Carbohydrates:** 35g
- **Fat:** 22g
- **Fiber:** 5g
- **Sodium:** 600mg

Enjoy your healthy and flavorful Grilled Chicken Pesto Panini!

Mediterranean Tuna Wrap

Prep Time: **10 mins** | Cooking Time: **None**
Yield: **4 portions**

INGREDIENTS:

- 2 cans tuna, drained
- 1/4 cup Greek yogurt
- 2 tbsp olive oil
- 1 tbsp lemon juice
- 1/4 cup red onion, chopped
- 1/4 cup cucumber, diced
- 1/4 cup kalamata olives, sliced
- 4 whole wheat tortillas
- Salt and pepper to taste

INSTRUCTIONS:

1. **Prepare Filling:**
   - Mix tuna, yogurt, olive oil, lemon juice, onion, cucumber, olives, salt, and pepper.
2. **Assemble Wraps:**
   - Spread filling on tortillas and roll up.
3. **Serve:**
   - Serve immediately.

NUTRITIONAL INFORMATION (PER SERVING):

- **Calories:** 300
- **Protein:** 25g
- **Carbohydrates:** 30g
- **Fat:** 10g
- **Fiber:** 4g
- **Sodium:** 400mg

Enjoy your healthy and flavorful Mediterranean Tuna Wrap!

Shrimp and Avocado Sandwich

Prep Time: **10 mins** | Cooking Time: **5 mins**
Yield: **4 portions**

INGREDIENTS:

- 1 lb shrimp, cooked and peeled
- 2 avocados, sliced
- 8 slices whole grain bread
- 1/4 cup Greek yogurt
- 1 tbsp lemon juice
- 1/4 cup red onion, sliced
- Salt and pepper to taste
- **Optional:** fresh dill

INSTRUCTIONS:

1. **Prepare Shrimp:**
   - Mix shrimp with Greek yogurt, lemon juice, salt, and pepper.
2. **Assemble Sandwiches:**
   - Layer avocado slices and shrimp mixture on bread. Add red onion and dill if desired. Top with remaining bread slices.
3. **Serve:**
   - Serve immediately.

NUTRITIONAL INFORMATION (PER SERVING):

- **Calories:** 350
- **Protein:** 20g
- **Carbohydrates:** 30g
- **Fat:** 15g
- **Fiber:** 6g
- **Sodium:** 400mg

Enjoy your healthy and flavorful Shrimp and Avocado Sandwich!

Roasted Veggie Pita

Prep Time: **10 mins** | Cooking Time: **20 mins**
Yield: **4 portions**

INGREDIENTS:

- 2 zucchinis, sliced
- 1 bell pepper, sliced
- 1 red onion, sliced
- 2 tbsp olive oil
- 1 tsp oregano
- Salt and pepper to taste
- 4 whole wheat pitas
- 1/2 cup hummus

INSTRUCTIONS:

1. **Roast Veggies:**
   Toss veggies with olive oil, oregano, salt, and pepper. Roast at 400°F for 20 minutes.
2. **Assemble Pitas:**
   Spread hummus on pitas. Fill with roasted veggies.
3. **Serve:**
   Serve immediately.

NUTRITIONAL INFORMATION (PER SERVING):

- **Calories:** 300
- **Protein:** 8g
- **Carbohydrates:** 40g
- **Fat:** 12g
- **Fiber:** 7g
- **Sodium:** 400mg

Enjoy your healthy and flavorful Roasted Veggie Pita!

Greek Salad Pizza

Prep Time: **10 mins** | Cooking Time: **15 mins**
Yield: **4 portions**

INGREDIENTS:

- 1 whole wheat pizza crust
- 1 cup hummus
- 1 cup cherry tomatoes, halved
- 1/2 cucumber, sliced
- 1/4 red onion, sliced
- 1/4 cup kalamata olives, sliced
- 1/4 cup feta cheese, crumbled
- 2 tbsp olive oil
- 1 tsp oregano
- Salt and pepper to taste

INSTRUCTIONS:

1. **Preheat Oven:**
   Preheat oven to 425°F.
2. **Prepare Pizza:**
   Spread hummus on pizza crust. Top with tomatoes, cucumber, onion, olives, and feta. Drizzle with olive oil and sprinkle with oregano, salt, and pepper.
3. **Bake:**
   Bake for 15 minutes.
4. **Serve:**
   Serve immediately.

NUTRITIONAL INFORMATION (PER SERVING):

- **Calories:** 350
- **Protein:** 12g
- **Carbohydrates:** 45g
- **Fat:** 15g
- **Fiber:** 6g
- **Sodium:** 600mg

Enjoy your healthy and flavorful Greek Salad Pizza!

Turkey and Hummus Wrap

Prep Time: **10 mins** | Cooking Time: **None**
Yield: **4 portions**

INGREDIENTS:

- 4 whole wheat tortillas
- 1 cup hummus
- 8 oz turkey breast, sliced
- 1 cup spinach leaves
- 1/2 cucumber, sliced
- 1/4 cup red onion, sliced
- Salt and pepper to taste

INSTRUCTIONS:

1. **Assemble Wraps:**
    - Spread hummus on tortillas. Layer with turkey, spinach, cucumber, and onion. Season with salt and pepper.
2. **Wrap:**
    - Roll up tortillas tightly.
3. **Serve:**
    - Serve immediately.

NUTRITIONAL INFORMATION (PER SERVING):

- **Calories:** 300
- **Protein:** 20g
- **Carbohydrates:** 35g
- **Fat:** 10g
- **Fiber:** 6g
- **Sodium:** 450mg

Enjoy your healthy and flavorful Turkey and Hummus Wrap!

Spinach and Feta Flatbread

Prep Time: **10 mins** | Cooking Time: **15 mins**
Yield: **4 portions**

INGREDIENTS:

- 2 whole wheat flatbreads
- 1 cup spinach, chopped
- 1/2 cup feta cheese, crumbled
- 2 tbsp olive oil
- 1 clove garlic, minced
- 1/4 tsp oregano
- Salt and pepper to taste

INSTRUCTIONS:

1. **Preheat Oven:**
    - Preheat oven to 400°F.
2. **Prepare Topping:**
    - Sauté garlic in olive oil until fragrant. Add spinach, cook until wilted. Season with oregano, salt, and pepper.
3. **Assemble Flatbreads:**
    - Spread spinach mixture on flatbreads. Sprinkle with feta cheese.
4. **Bake:**
    - Bake for 10-15 minutes until flatbreads are crisp.
5. **Serve:**
    - Serve immediately.

NUTRITIONAL INFORMATION (PER SERVING):

- **Calories:** 250
- **Protein:** 8g
- **Carbohydrates:** 25g
- **Fat:** 14g
- **Fiber:** 4g
- **Sodium:** 400mg

Enjoy your healthy and flavorful Spinach and Feta Flatbread!

Lamb Gyro

Prep Time: **10 mins** | Cooking Time: **15 mins**
Yield: **4 portions**

INGREDIENTS:

- 1 lb ground lamb
- 1 tsp oregano
- 1 tsp cumin
- 2 cloves garlic, minced
- Salt and pepper to taste
- 4 whole wheat pitas
- 1 cup tzatziki sauce
- 1 cup lettuce, shredded
- 1 tomato, sliced
- 1/4 red onion, sliced

INSTRUCTIONS:

1. **Cook Lamb:**
   - Sauté lamb with oregano, cumin, garlic, salt, and pepper until fully cooked.
2. **Assemble Gyros:**
   - Fill pitas with lamb, tzatziki, lettuce, tomato, and onion.
3. **Serve:**
   - Serve immediately.

NUTRITIONAL INFORMATION (PER SERVING):

- **Calories:** 450
- **Protein:** 25g
- **Carbohydrates:** 35g
- **Fat:** 22g
- **Fiber:** 5g
- **Sodium:** 600mg

Enjoy your healthy and flavorful Lamb Gyro!

Grilled Halloumi Wrap

Prep Time: **10 mins** | Cooking Time: **10 mins**
Yield: **4 portions**

INGREDIENTS:

- 8 oz halloumi cheese, sliced
- 4 whole wheat tortillas
- 1 cup lettuce, shredded
- 1/2 cup cherry tomatoes, halved
- 1/4 cucumber, sliced
- 2 tbsp olive oil
- 1 tbsp lemon juice
- Salt and pepper to taste

INSTRUCTIONS:

1. **Grill Halloumi:**
   - Grill halloumi slices on a skillet until golden, about 2-3 minutes per side.
2. **Assemble Wraps:**
   - Place grilled halloumi on tortillas. Add lettuce, tomatoes, and cucumber. Drizzle with olive oil and lemon juice. Season with salt and pepper.
3. **Serve:**
   - Roll up tortillas and serve immediately.

NUTRITIONAL INFORMATION (PER SERVING):

- **Calories:** 350
- **Protein:** 15g
- **Carbohydrates:** 30g
- **Fat:** 18g
- **Fiber:** 4g
- **Sodium:** 500mg

Enjoy your healthy and flavorful Grilled Halloumi Wrap!

Italian Sub with Olive Tapenade

Prep Time: **10 mins** | Cooking Time: **None**
Yield: **4 portions**

INGREDIENTS:

- 4 whole grain sub rolls
- 8 oz deli turkey or ham, sliced
- 1 cup lettuce, shredded
- 1 tomato, sliced
- 1/4 red onion, sliced
- 1/4 cup olive tapenade
- 2 tbsp olive oil
- 1 tbsp balsamic vinegar
- Salt and pepper to taste

INSTRUCTIONS:

1. **Prepare Subs:**
   - Spread olive tapenade on sub rolls. Layer with turkey or ham, lettuce, tomato, and onion.
2. **Dress:**
   - Drizzle with olive oil and balsamic vinegar. Season with salt and pepper.
3. **Serve:**
   - Serve immediately.

NUTRITIONAL INFORMATION (PER SERVING):

- **Calories:** 400
- **Protein:** 20g
- **Carbohydrates:** 40g
- **Fat:** 18g
- **Fiber:** 6g
- **Sodium:** 700mg

Enjoy your healthy and flavorful Italian Sub with Olive Tapenade!

Roasted Beet and Goat Cheese Sandwich

Prep Time: **10 mins** | Cooking Time: **20 mins**
Yield: **4 portions**

INGREDIENTS:

- 4 whole grain rolls
- 2 large beets, roasted and sliced
- 4 oz goat cheese, crumbled
- 1 cup arugula
- 2 tbsp olive oil
- 1 tbsp balsamic vinegar
- Salt and pepper to taste

INSTRUCTIONS:

1. **Roast Beets:**
   - Roast beets at 400°F for 20 minutes. Cool and slice.
2. **Assemble Sandwiches:**
   - Spread goat cheese on rolls. Layer with beets and arugula.
3. **Dress:**
   - Drizzle with olive oil and balsamic vinegar. Season with salt and pepper.
4. **Serve:**
   - Serve immediately.

NUTRITIONAL INFORMATION (PER SERVING):

- **Calories:** 300
- **Protein:** 10g
- **Carbohydrates:** 40g
- **Fat:** 12g
- **Fiber:** 6g
- **Sodium:** 400mg

Enjoy your healthy and flavorful Roasted Beet and Goat Cheese Sandwich!

Mediterranean Turkey Club

Prep Time: **10 mins** | Cooking Time: **None**
Yield: **4 portions**

INGREDIENTS:

- 8 slices whole grain bread
- 8 oz turkey breast, sliced
- 1 avocado, sliced
- 1 tomato, sliced
- 1/4 cup hummus
- 1 cup spinach leaves
- 2 tbsp olive oil
- Salt and pepper to taste

INSTRUCTIONS:

1. **Assemble Sandwiches:**
   Spread hummus on bread slices. Layer with turkey, avocado, tomato, and spinach.
2. **Dress:**
   Drizzle with olive oil. Season with salt and pepper.
3. **Top:**
   Place remaining bread slices on top.
4. **Serve:**
   Serve immediately.

NUTRITIONAL INFORMATION (PER SERVING):

- **Calories:** 350
- **Protein:** 20g
- **Carbohydrates:** 35g
- **Fat:** 15g
- **Fiber:** 8g
- **Sodium:** 450mg

Enjoy your healthy and flavorful Mediterranean Turkey Club!

Hummus and Roasted Red Pepper Sandwich

Prep Time: **10 mins** | Cooking Time: **None**
Yield: **4 portions**

INGREDIENTS:

- 8 slices whole grain bread
- 1 cup hummus
- 2 roasted red peppers, sliced
- 1 cup arugula
- 1/4 red onion, thinly sliced
- 2 tbsp olive oil
- Salt and pepper to taste

INSTRUCTIONS:

1. **Assemble Sandwiches:**
   Spread hummus on bread slices. Layer with roasted red peppers, arugula, and red onion.
2. **Dress:**
   Drizzle with olive oil. Season with salt and pepper.
3. **Top:**
   Place remaining bread slices on top.
4. **Serve:**
   Serve immediately.

NUTRITIONAL INFORMATION (PER SERVING):

- **Calories:** 300
- **Protein:** 10g
- **Carbohydrates:** 40g
- **Fat:** 12g
- **Fiber:** 8g
- **Sodium:** 400mg

Enjoy your healthy and flavorful Hummus and Roasted Red Pepper Sandwich!

Portobello Mushroom Burger

Prep Time: **10 mins** | Cooking Time: **10 mins**
Yield: **4 portions**

INGREDIENTS:

- 4 large Portobello mushrooms
- 2 tbsp olive oil
- 1 tbsp balsamic vinegar
- 1 tsp garlic powder
- Salt and pepper to taste
- 4 whole grain buns
- 1 avocado, sliced
- 1 tomato, sliced
- 1 cup arugula

INSTRUCTIONS:

1. **Marinate Mushrooms:**
   - Brush mushrooms with olive oil, balsamic vinegar, garlic powder, salt, and pepper.
2. **Grill Mushrooms:**
   - Grill mushrooms on a skillet for 5 minutes per side.
3. **Assemble Burgers:**
   - Place grilled mushrooms on buns. Top with avocado, tomato, and arugula.
4. **Serve:**
   - Serve immediately.

NUTRITIONAL INFORMATION (PER SERVING):

- **Calories:** 300
- **Protein:** 8g
- **Carbohydrates:** 35g
- **Fat:** 16g
- **Fiber:** 6g
- **Sodium:** 400mg

Enjoy your healthy and flavorful Portobello Mushroom Burger!

Smoked Salmon Bagel with Cream Cheese

Prep Time: **5 mins** | Cooking Time: **None**
Yield: **4 portions**

INGREDIENTS:

- 4 whole grain bagels
- 8 oz smoked salmon
- 8 oz cream cheese
- 1/2 red onion, thinly sliced
- 1/2 cucumber, sliced
- 1 tbsp capers
- Fresh dill, for garnish
- Salt and pepper to taste

INSTRUCTIONS:

1. **Assemble Bagels:**
   - Spread cream cheese on each bagel half.
   - Layer with smoked salmon, red onion, cucumber, and capers.
   - Garnish with fresh dill, salt, and pepper.
2. **Serve:**
   - Serve immediately.

NUTRITIONAL INFORMATION (PER SERVING):

- **Calories:** 400
- **Protein:** 18g
- **Carbohydrates:** 45g
- **Fat:** 18g
- **Fiber:** 5g
- **Sodium:** 800mg

Enjoy your healthy and flavorful Smoked Salmon Bagel with Cream Cheese!

CHAPTER 11. BEANS AND GRAINS

Quinoa Tabbouleh

Prep Time: **10 mins** | Cooking Time: **15 mins**
Yield: **4 portions**

INGREDIENTS:

- 1 cup quinoa
- 2 cups water
- 1 cup parsley, chopped
- 1/2 cup mint, chopped
- 1/2 cup cherry tomatoes, halved
- 1 cucumber, diced
- 1/4 cup olive oil
- 1/4 cup lemon juice
- Salt and pepper to taste

INSTRUCTIONS:

1. **Cook Quinoa:**
   - Boil quinoa in water for 15 minutes. Let cool.
2. **Mix Ingredients:**
   - Combine quinoa, parsley, mint, tomatoes, cucumber, olive oil, lemon juice, salt, and pepper.
3. **Serve:**
   - Serve chilled.

NUTRITIONAL INFORMATION (PER SERVING):

- **Calories:** 200
- **Protein:** 5g
- **Carbohydrates:** 25g
- **Fat:** 10g
- **Fiber:** 5g
- **Sodium:** 100mg

Enjoy your healthy and flavorful Quinoa Tabbouleh!

Lentil and Vegetable Stew

Prep Time: **10 mins** | Cooking Time: **40 mins**
Yield: **4 portions**

INGREDIENTS:

- 1 cup lentils
- 1 onion, chopped
- 2 cloves garlic, minced
- 2 carrots, chopped
- 2 celery stalks, chopped
- 1 zucchini, chopped
- 1 can diced tomatoes (14.5 oz)
- 4 cups vegetable broth
- 1 tsp cumin
- 1 tsp oregano
- 2 tbsp olive oil
- Salt and pepper to taste
- Fresh parsley, for garnish

INSTRUCTIONS:

1. **Sauté Vegetables:**
   - In a large pot, heat olive oil. Sauté onion, garlic, carrots, and celery until tender.
2. **Cook Stew:**
   - Add lentils, zucchini, tomatoes, broth, cumin, and oregano. Simmer for 30 minutes.
3. **Season:**
   - Season with salt and pepper.
4. **Serve:**
   - Garnish with fresh parsley and serve.

NUTRITIONAL INFORMATION (PER SERVING):

- **Calories:** 250
- **Protein:** 12g
- **Carbohydrates:** 35g
- **Fat:** 8g
- **Fiber:** 12g
- **Sodium:** 600mg

Enjoy your healthy and flavorful Lentil and Vegetable Stew!

Chickpea and Spinach Curry

Prep Time: **10 mins** | Cooking Time: **20 mins**
Yield: **4 portions**

INGREDIENTS:

- 2 cans chickpeas, drained and rinsed
- 1 onion, chopped
- 3 cloves garlic, minced
- 1 can diced tomatoes (14.5 oz)
- 1 cup coconut milk
- 4 cups spinach, chopped
- 2 tbsp olive oil
- 1 tbsp curry powder
- 1 tsp cumin
- Salt and pepper to taste
- Fresh cilantro, for garnish

INSTRUCTIONS:

1. **Sauté Onions:**
   - In a skillet, heat olive oil. Sauté onion and garlic until soft.
2. **Cook Curry:**
   - Add curry powder and cumin, cook for 1 minute. Add chickpeas, tomatoes, and coconut milk. Simmer for 15 minutes.
3. **Add Spinach:**
   - Stir in spinach until wilted. Season with salt and pepper.
4. **Serve:**
   - Garnish with fresh cilantro and serve.

NUTRITIONAL INFORMATION (PER SERVING):

- **Calories:** 300
- **Protein:** 10g
- **Carbohydrates:** 35g
- **Fat:** 14g
- **Fiber:** 10g
- **Sodium:** 500mg

Enjoy your healthy and flavorful Chickpea and Spinach Curry!

Farro Salad with Roasted Vegetables

Prep Time: **10 mins** | Cooking Time: **30 mins**
Yield: **4 portions**

INGREDIENTS:

- 1 cup farro
- 2 cups water
- 1 zucchini, chopped
- 1 red bell pepper, chopped
- 1 eggplant, chopped
- 2 tbsp olive oil
- 1 tsp oregano
- Salt and pepper to taste
- 1/4 cup feta cheese, crumbled
- 2 tbsp fresh parsley, chopped

INSTRUCTIONS:

1. **Cook Farro:**
   - Boil farro in water for 20 minutes. Drain and cool.
2. **Roast Vegetables:**
   - Toss zucchini, bell pepper, and eggplant with olive oil, oregano, salt, and pepper. Roast at 400°F for 20 minutes.
3. **Combine Ingredients:**
   - Mix farro, roasted vegetables, feta, and parsley.
4. **Serve:**
   - Serve immediately.

NUTRITIONAL INFORMATION (PER SERVING):

- **Calories:** 300
- **Protein:** 10g
- **Carbohydrates:** 40g
- **Fat:** 12g
- **Fiber:** 8g
- **Sodium:** 350mg

Enjoy your healthy and flavorful Farro Salad with Roasted Vegetables!

CHAPTER 11. BEANS AND GRAINS

White Bean and Kale Soup

Prep Time: **10 mins** | Cooking Time: **20 mins**
Yield: **4 portions**

INGREDIENTS:

- 2 cans white beans, drained and rinsed
- 1 onion, chopped
- 3 cloves garlic, minced
- 4 cups kale, chopped
- 4 cups vegetable broth
- 2 tbsp olive oil
- 1 tsp thyme
- Salt and pepper to taste

INSTRUCTIONS:

1. **Sauté Onions:**
   - In a pot, heat olive oil. Sauté onion and garlic until soft.
2. **Cook Soup:**
   - Add beans, broth, and thyme. Simmer for 10 minutes. Add kale, cook until wilted.
3. **Season:**
   - Season with salt and pepper.
4. **Serve:**
   - Serve immediately.

NUTRITIONAL INFORMATION (PER SERVING):

- **Calories:** 250
- **Protein:** 10g
- **Carbohydrates:** 35g
- **Fat:** 8g
- **Fiber:** 10g
- **Sodium:** 500mg

Enjoy your healthy and flavorful White Bean and Kale Soup!

Mediterranean Barley Risotto

Prep Time: **10 mins** | Cooking Time: **30 mins**
Yield: **4 portions**

INGREDIENTS:

- 1 cup pearl barley
- 4 cups vegetable broth
- 1 onion, chopped
- 2 cloves garlic, minced
- 1 cup cherry tomatoes, halved
- 1/2 cup kalamata olives, sliced
- 2 tbsp olive oil
- 1/4 cup Parmesan cheese, grated
- 1/4 cup fresh basil, chopped
- Salt and pepper to taste

INSTRUCTIONS:

1. **Sauté Onions:**
   - In a skillet, heat olive oil. Sauté onion and garlic until soft.
2. **Cook Barley:**
   - Add barley, stir for 2 minutes. Gradually add broth, simmer until barley is tender, about 25 minutes.
3. **Add Ingredients:**
   - Stir in tomatoes, olives, and Parmesan. Cook until heated through. Season with salt and pepper.
4. **Serve:**
   - Garnish with basil and serve.

NUTRITIONAL INFORMATION (PER SERVING):

- **Calories:** 300
- **Protein:** 10g
- **Carbohydrates:** 45g
- **Fat:** 10g
- **Fiber:** 8g
- **Sodium:** 400mg

Enjoy your healthy and flavorful Mediterranean Barley Risotto!

Bulgur Wheat Salad

Prep Time: **10 mins** | Cooking Time: **15 mins**
Yield: **4 portions**

INGREDIENTS:

- 1 cup bulgur wheat
- 1 1/2 cups boiling water
- 1 cup cherry tomatoes, halved
- 1 cucumber, diced
- 1/4 cup parsley, chopped
- 1/4 cup mint, chopped
- 1/4 cup olive oil
- 2 tbsp lemon juice
- Salt and pepper to taste

INSTRUCTIONS:

1. **Prepare Bulgur:**
   - Place bulgur in a bowl, pour boiling water over it. Cover and let sit for 15 minutes. Fluff with a fork.
2. **Combine Ingredients:**
   - Mix bulgur with tomatoes, cucumber, parsley, mint, olive oil, lemon juice, salt, and pepper.
3. **Serve:**
   - Serve immediately or chilled.

NUTRITIONAL INFORMATION (PER SERVING):

- **Calories:** 220
- **Protein:** 5g
- **Carbohydrates:** 30g
- **Fat:** 10g
- **Fiber:** 7g
- **Sodium:** 200mg

Enjoy your healthy and flavorful Bulgur Wheat Salad!

Brown Rice Pilaf with Vegetables

Prep Time: **10 mins** | Cooking Time: **30 mins**
Yield: **4 portions**

INGREDIENTS:

- 1 cup brown rice
- 2 cups vegetable broth
- 1 onion, chopped
- 2 cloves garlic, minced
- 1 carrot, diced
- 1 bell pepper, diced
- 1 zucchini, diced
- 2 tbsp olive oil
- 1 tsp thyme
- Salt and pepper to taste

INSTRUCTIONS:

1. **Sauté Vegetables:**
   - In a skillet, heat olive oil. Sauté onion, garlic, carrot, bell pepper, and zucchini until tender.
2. **Cook Rice:**
   - Add brown rice, thyme, vegetable broth, salt, and pepper. Bring to a boil, then simmer for 30 minutes or until rice is cooked.
3. **Serve:**
   - Fluff rice with a fork and serve.

NUTRITIONAL INFORMATION (PER SERVING):

- **Calories:** 250
- **Protein:** 5g
- **Carbohydrates:** 40g
- **Fat:** 8g
- **Fiber:** 5g
- **Sodium:** 300mg

Enjoy your healthy and flavorful Brown Rice Pilaf with Vegetables!

Red Lentil Soup with Lemon

Prep Time: **10 mins** | Cooking Time: **20 mins**
Yield: **4 portions**

INGREDIENTS:

- 1 cup red lentils
- 1 onion, chopped
- 2 cloves garlic, minced
- 1 carrot, diced
- 1 celery stalk, diced
- 4 cups vegetable broth
- 1 tsp cumin
- 1/2 tsp turmeric
- 2 tbsp olive oil
- Juice of 1 lemon
- Salt and pepper to taste

INSTRUCTIONS:

1. **Sauté Vegetables:**
   - In a pot, heat olive oil. Sauté onion, garlic, carrot, and celery until tender.
2. **Cook Soup:**
   - Add lentils, broth, cumin, and turmeric. Bring to a boil, then simmer for 20 minutes.
3. **Add Lemon:**
   - Stir in lemon juice. Season with salt and pepper.
4. **Serve:**
   - Serve immediately.

NUTRITIONAL INFORMATION (PER SERVING):

- **Calories:** 200
- **Protein:** 10g
- **Carbohydrates:** 30g
- **Fat:** 6g
- **Fiber:** 10g
- **Sodium:** 400mg

Enjoy your healthy and flavorful Red Lentil Soup with Lemon!

Black Bean and Corn Salad

Prep Time: **10 mins** | Cooking Time: **None**
Yield: **4 portions**

INGREDIENTS:

- 1 can black beans, drained and rinsed
- 1 cup corn kernels (fresh or canned)
- 1 red bell pepper, diced
- 1/4 red onion, diced
- 1/4 cup cilantro, chopped
- 2 tbsp olive oil
- 1 tbsp lime juice
- Salt and pepper to taste

INSTRUCTIONS:

1. **Combine Ingredients:**
   - Mix beans, corn, bell pepper, onion, and cilantro in a bowl.
2. **Dress Salad:**
   - Add olive oil, lime juice, salt, and pepper. Toss to combine.
3. **Serve:**
   - Serve immediately.

NUTRITIONAL INFORMATION (PER SERVING):

- **Calories:** 180
- **Protein:** 6g
- **Carbohydrates:** 28g
- **Fat:** 6g
- **Fiber:** 7g
- **Sodium:** 300mg

Enjoy your healthy and flavorful Black Bean and Corn Salad!

White Bean and Spinach Stew

Prep Time: **10 mins** | Cooking Time: **20 mins**
Yield: **4 portions**

INGREDIENTS:

- 2 cans white beans, drained and rinsed
- 1 onion, chopped
- 2 cloves garlic, minced
- 4 cups spinach, chopped
- 4 cups vegetable broth
- 2 tbsp olive oil
- 1 tsp thyme
- Salt and pepper to taste

INSTRUCTIONS:

1. **Sauté Onions:**
   - In a pot, heat olive oil. Sauté onion and garlic until soft.
2. **Cook Stew:**
   - Add beans, broth, and thyme. Simmer for 15 minutes. Add spinach and cook until wilted.
3. **Season:**
   - Season with salt and pepper.
4. **Serve:**
   - Serve immediately.

NUTRITIONAL INFORMATION (PER SERVING):

- **Calories:** 220
- **Protein:** 10g
- **Carbohydrates:** 30g
- **Fat:** 8g
- **Fiber:** 8g
- **Sodium:** 400mg

Enjoy your healthy and flavorful White Bean and Spinach Stew!

Mediterranean Spelt Salad

Prep Time: **10 mins** | Cooking Time: **30 mins**
Yield: **4 portions**

INGREDIENTS:

- 1 cup spelt
- 2 cups water
- 1 cup cherry tomatoes, halved
- 1 cucumber, diced
- 1/4 cup kalamata olives, sliced
- 1/4 cup feta cheese, crumbled
- 2 tbsp olive oil
- 1 tbsp lemon juice
- 1 tbsp fresh parsley, chopped
- Salt and pepper to taste

INSTRUCTIONS:

1. **Cook Spelt:**
   - Boil spelt in water for 30 minutes. Drain and let cool.
2. **Combine Ingredients:**
   - Mix spelt with tomatoes, cucumber, olives, feta, olive oil, lemon juice, parsley, salt, and pepper.
3. **Serve:**
   - Serve immediately or chilled.

NUTRITIONAL INFORMATION (PER SERVING):

- **Calories:** 250
- **Protein:** 8g
- **Carbohydrates:** 35g
- **Fat:** 10g
- **Fiber:** 7g
- **Sodium:** 350mg

Enjoy your healthy and flavorful Mediterranean Spelt Salad!

Three-Bean Salad with Lemon Vinaigrette

Prep Time: **10 mins** | Cooking Time: **None**
Yield: **4 portions**

INGREDIENTS:

- 1 can chickpeas, drained and rinsed
- 1 can kidney beans, drained and rinsed
- 1 can green beans, drained and rinsed
- 1/4 red onion, diced
- 1/4 cup fresh parsley, chopped
- 2 tbsp olive oil
- 2 tbsp lemon juice
- 1 tsp Dijon mustard
- Salt and pepper to taste

INSTRUCTIONS:

1. **Combine Beans:**
   - Mix chickpeas, kidney beans, green beans, onion, and parsley in a bowl.
2. **Prepare Vinaigrette:**
   - Whisk olive oil, lemon juice, mustard, salt, and pepper in a small bowl.
3. **Dress Salad:**
   - Pour vinaigrette over beans and toss to combine.
4. **Serve:**
   - Serve immediately or chilled.

NUTRITIONAL INFORMATION (PER SERVING):

- **Calories:** 200
- **Protein:** 8g
- **Carbohydrates:** 30g
- **Fat:** 6g
- **Fiber:** 8g
- **Sodium:** 300mg

Enjoy your healthy and flavorful Three-Bean Salad with Lemon Vinaigrette!

Red Lentil and Spinach Dhal

Prep Time: **10 mins** | Cooking Time: **20 mins**
Yield: **4 portions**

INGREDIENTS:

- 1 cup red lentils
- 4 cups spinach, chopped
- 1 onion, chopped
- 2 cloves garlic, minced
- 1 tsp ginger, minced
- 1 tsp cumin
- 1 tsp turmeric
- 4 cups vegetable broth
- 2 tbsp olive oil
- Salt and pepper to taste

INSTRUCTIONS:

1. **Sauté Aromatics:**
   - In a pot, heat olive oil. Sauté onion, garlic, and ginger until soft.
2. **Cook Lentils:**
   - Add lentils, cumin, turmeric, and broth. Simmer for 15 minutes.
3. **Add Spinach:**
   - Stir in spinach until wilted. Season with salt and pepper.
4. **Serve:**
   - Serve immediately.

NUTRITIONAL INFORMATION (PER SERVING):

- **Calories:** 220
- **Protein:** 10g
- **Carbohydrates:** 30g
- **Fat:** 7g
- **Fiber:** 10g
- **Sodium:** 400mg

Enjoy your healthy and flavorful Red Lentil and Spinach Dhal!

Mediterranean Bulgur Pilaf

Prep Time: **10 mins** | Cooking Time: **15 mins**
Yield: **4 portions**

INGREDIENTS:

- 1 cup bulgur wheat
- 2 cups vegetable broth
- 1 onion, chopped
- 1 bell pepper, chopped
- 1 tomato, chopped
- 2 tbsp olive oil
- 1 tsp cumin
- 1/4 cup fresh parsley, chopped
- Salt and pepper to taste

INSTRUCTIONS:

1. **Sauté Vegetables:**
   - In a skillet, heat olive oil. Sauté onion and bell pepper until soft.
2. **Cook Bulgur:**
   - Add bulgur, broth, tomato, and cumin. Bring to a boil, then simmer for 10 minutes.
3. **Finish Pilaf:**
   - Stir in parsley, salt, and pepper.
4. **Serve:**
   - Serve immediately.

NUTRITIONAL INFORMATION (PER SERVING):

- **Calories:** 200
- **Protein:** 5g
- **Carbohydrates:** 30g
- **Fat:** 7g
- **Fiber:** 6g
- **Sodium:** 350mg

Enjoy your healthy and flavorful Mediterranean Bulgur Pilaf!

Rice and Bean Stuffed Peppers

Prep Time: **10 mins** | Cooking Time: **30 mins**
Yield: **4 portions**

INGREDIENTS:

- 4 bell peppers, tops cut off and seeds removed
- 1 cup cooked brown rice
- 1 can black beans, drained and rinsed
- 1 tomato, chopped
- 1/2 onion, chopped
- 2 cloves garlic, minced
- 1 tsp cumin
- 1 tsp oregano
- 2 tbsp olive oil
- Salt and pepper to taste

INSTRUCTIONS:

1. **Preheat Oven:**
   - Preheat oven to 375°F.
2. **Sauté Vegetables:**
   - In a skillet, heat olive oil. Sauté onion and garlic until soft.
3. **Mix Filling:**
   - In a bowl, combine rice, beans, tomato, sautéed onion and garlic, cumin, oregano, salt, and pepper.
4. **Stuff Peppers:**
   - Fill bell peppers with the mixture.
5. **Bake:**
   - Place stuffed peppers in a baking dish and bake for 20 minutes.
6. **Serve:**
   - Serve immediately.

NUTRITIONAL INFORMATION (PER SERVING):

- **Calories:** 250
- **Protein:** 7g
- **Carbohydrates:** 40g
- **Fat:** 8g
- **Fiber:** 8g
- **Sodium:** 350mg

Enjoy your healthy and flavorful Rice and Bean Stuffed Peppers!

CHAPTER 12. STAPLES, SAUCES, DIPS, AND DRESSINGS

Tzatziki Sauce

Prep Time: **10 mins** | Cooking Time: **None**
Yield: **4 portions**

INGREDIENTS:

- 1 cup Greek yogurt
- 1 cucumber, grated and drained
- 2 cloves garlic, minced
- 1 tbsp olive oil
- 1 tbsp lemon juice
- 1 tbsp fresh dill, chopped
- Salt and pepper to taste

INSTRUCTIONS:

1. **Mix Ingredients:**
   - Combine yogurt, cucumber, garlic, olive oil, lemon juice, dill, salt, and pepper in a bowl.
2. **Chill:**
   - Refrigerate for at least 30 minutes before serving.

NUTRITIONAL INFORMATION (PER SERVING):

- **Calories:** 60
- **Protein:** 3g
- **Carbohydrates:** 4g
- **Fat:** 4g
- **Fiber:** 0g
- **Sodium:** 80mg

Enjoy your healthy and flavorful Tzatziki Sauce!

Harissa Paste

Prep Time: **10 mins** | Cooking Time: **None**
Yield: **4 portions**

INGREDIENTS:

- 4 dried chili peppers, soaked and seeded
- 2 cloves garlic
- 1 tsp cumin seeds
- 1 tsp coriander seeds
- 1 tsp caraway seeds
- 2 tbsp olive oil
- 1 tbsp lemon juice
- Salt to taste

INSTRUCTIONS:

1. **Blend Ingredients:**
   - Combine soaked chili peppers, garlic, cumin, coriander, caraway, olive oil, lemon juice, and salt in a blender. Blend until smooth.

NUTRITIONAL INFORMATION (PER SERVING):

- **Calories:** 60
- **Protein:** 1g
- **Carbohydrates:** 2g
- **Fat:** 6g
- **Fiber:** 1g
- **Sodium:** 150mg

Enjoy your healthy and flavorful Harissa Paste!

Mediterranean Herb Blend

Prep Time: **5 mins** | Cooking Time: **None**
Yield: **4 portions**

INGREDIENTS:

- 2 tbsp dried oregano
- 2 tbsp dried thyme
- 2 tbsp dried basil
- 1 tbsp dried rosemary
- 1 tbsp dried parsley
- 1 tbsp dried mint
- 1 tsp garlic powder
- 1 tsp onion powder

INSTRUCTIONS:

1. **Mix Ingredients:**
   Combine all herbs and spices in a bowl. Mix well and store in an airtight container.

NUTRITIONAL INFORMATION (PER SERVING):

- **Calories:** 5
- **Protein:** 0g
- **Carbohydrates:** 1g
- **Fat:** 0g
- **Fiber:** 0g
- **Sodium:** 0mg

Enjoy your healthy and flavorful Mediterranean Herb Blend!

Mint Yogurt Sauce

Prep Time: **5 mins** | Cooking Time: **None**
Yield: **4 portions**

INGREDIENTS:

- 1 cup Greek yogurt
- 2 tbsp fresh mint, chopped
- 1 tbsp lemon juice
- 1 clove garlic, minced
- Salt and pepper to taste

INSTRUCTIONS:

1. **Mix Ingredients:**
   Combine all ingredients in a bowl and mix well.

NUTRITIONAL INFORMATION (PER SERVING):

- **Calories:** 50
- **Protein:** 4g
- **Carbohydrates:** 3g
- **Fat:** 2g
- **Fiber:** 0g
- **Sodium:** 60mg

Enjoy your healthy and flavorful Mint Yogurt Sauce!

Red Wine Vinaigrette

Prep Time: **5 mins** | Cooking Time: **None**
Yield: **4 portions**

INGREDIENTS:

- 1/4 cup red wine vinegar
- 1/2 cup olive oil
- 1 tsp Dijon mustard
- 1 clove garlic, minced
- Salt and pepper to taste

INSTRUCTIONS:

1. **Mix Ingredients:**
   - Whisk together vinegar, olive oil, mustard, garlic, salt, and pepper in a bowl.

NUTRITIONAL INFORMATION (PER SERVING):

- **Calories:** 120
- **Protein:** 0g
- **Carbohydrates:** 0g
- **Fat:** 14g
- **Fiber:** 0g
- **Sodium:** 60mg

Enjoy your healthy and flavorful Red Wine Vinaigrette!

Chimichurri Sauce

Prep Time: **5 mins** | Cooking Time: **None**
Yield: **4 portions**

INGREDIENTS:

- 1 cup fresh parsley, chopped
- 1/2 cup olive oil
- 1/4 cup red wine vinegar
- 1 tbsp fresh oregano, chopped
- 2 cloves garlic, minced
- 1/2 tsp red pepper flakes (optional)
- Salt and pepper to taste

INSTRUCTIONS:

1. **Mix Ingredients:**
   - Combine all ingredients in a bowl and mix well.

NUTRITIONAL INFORMATION (PER SERVING):

- **Calories:** 120
- **Protein:** 1g
- **Carbohydrates:** 1g
- **Fat:** 14g
- **Fiber:** 1g
- **Sodium:** 50mg

Enjoy your healthy and flavorful Chimichurri Sauce!

Artichoke and Olive Tapenade

Prep Time: **5 mins** | Cooking Time: **None**
Yield: **4 portions**

INGREDIENTS:

- 1 cup artichoke hearts, drained
- 1/2 cup kalamata olives
- 2 cloves garlic
- 2 tbsp olive oil
- 1 tbsp lemon juice
- Salt and pepper to taste

INSTRUCTIONS:

1. **Blend Ingredients:**
   - Combine all ingredients in a blender. Blend until smooth.

NUTRITIONAL INFORMATION (PER SERVING):

- **Calories:** 100
- **Protein:** 1g
- **Carbohydrates:** 2g
- **Fat:** 10g
- **Fiber:** 1g
- **Sodium:** 300mg

Enjoy your healthy and flavorful Artichoke and Olive Tapenade!

Sun-Dried Tomato and Basil Spread

Prep Time: **5 mins** | Cooking Time: **None**
Yield: **4 portions**

INGREDIENTS:

- 1 cup sun-dried tomatoes (packed in oil), drained
- 1/2 cup fresh basil leaves
- 1/4 cup olive oil
- 2 cloves garlic
- Salt and pepper to taste

INSTRUCTIONS:

1. **Blend Ingredients:**
   - Combine all ingredients in a blender. Blend until smooth.

NUTRITIONAL INFORMATION (PER SERVING):

- **Calories:** 110
- **Protein:** 1g
- **Carbohydrates:** 3g
- **Fat:** 10g
- **Fiber:** 1g
- **Sodium:** 150mg

Enjoy your healthy and flavorful Sun-Dried Tomato and Basil Spread!

CHAPTER 13. DESERT

Greek Yogurt with Honey and Walnuts

Prep Time: **5 mins** | Cooking Time: **None**
Yield: **4 portions**

INGREDIENTS:

- 2 cups Greek yogurt
- 1/4 cup honey
- 1/4 cup walnuts, chopped
- 1/2 tsp cinnamon (optional)

INSTRUCTIONS:

1. **Assemble:**
   - Divide yogurt into 4 bowls. Drizzle with honey and sprinkle with walnuts and cinnamon.

NUTRITIONAL INFORMATION (PER SERVING):

- **Calories:** 200
- **Protein:** 10g
- **Carbohydrates:** 25g
- **Fat:** 7g
- **Fiber:** 1g
- **Sodium:** 50mg

Enjoy your healthy and flavorful Greek Yogurt with Honey and Walnuts!

Orange Blossom Semolina Cake

Prep Time: **15 mins** | Cooking Time: **30 mins**
Yield: **8 portions**

INGREDIENTS:

- 1 cup semolina
- 1 cup Greek yogurt
- 1/2 cup sugar
- 1/4 cup olive oil
- 1 tsp baking powder
- 2 tbsp orange blossom water
- Zest of 1 orange
- 1/4 cup honey

INSTRUCTIONS:

1. **Prcheat Oven:**
   - Preheat to 350°F (175°C).
2. **Mix Ingredients:**
   - Combine semolina, yogurt, sugar, olive oil, baking powder, orange blossom water, and orange zest in a bowl. Mix well.
3. **Bake:**
   - Pour into a greased baking dish. Bake for 30 minutes or until golden.
4. **Drizzle:**
   - Drizzle with honey while warm.

NUTRITIONAL INFORMATION (PER SERVING):

- **Calories:** 220
- **Protein:** 4g
- **Carbohydrates:** 30g
- **Fat:** 9g
- **Fiber:** 1g
- **Sodium:** 60mg

Enjoy your healthy and flavorful Orange Blossom Semolina Cake!

Date and Walnut Bars

Prep Time: **10 mins** | Cooking Time: **20 mins**
Yield: **8 portions**

INGREDIENTS:

- 1 cup dates, pitted and chopped
- 1 cup walnuts, chopped
- 1 cup oats
- 1/4 cup honey
- 1/4 cup olive oil
- 1 tsp cinnamon

INSTRUCTIONS:

1. **Preheat Oven:**
   - Preheat to 350°F (175°C).
2. **Mix Ingredients:**
   - Combine dates, walnuts, oats, honey, olive oil, and cinnamon in a bowl. Mix well.
3. **Bake:**
   - Press mixture into a greased baking dish. Bake for 20 minutes.
4. **Cool and Serve:**
   - Let cool before cutting into bars.

NUTRITIONAL INFORMATION (PER SERVING):

- **Calories:** 220
- **Protein:** 3g
- **Carbohydrates:** 28g
- **Fat:** 11g
- **Fiber:** 3g
- **Sodium:** 5mg

Enjoy your healthy and flavorful Date and Walnut Bars!

Honey Almond Biscotti

Prep Time: **10 mins** | Cooking Time: **30 mins**
Yield: **12 portions**

INGREDIENTS:

- 1 1/2 cups whole wheat flour
- 1/2 cup almonds, chopped
- 1/4 cup honey
- 1/4 cup olive oil
- 2 eggs
- 1 tsp baking powder
- 1 tsp vanilla extract

INSTRUCTIONS:

1. **Preheat Oven:**
   - Preheat to 350°F (175°C).
2. **Mix Ingredients:**
   - Combine flour, almonds, baking powder in a bowl. In another bowl, mix honey, olive oil, eggs, and vanilla. Combine wet and dry ingredients.
3. **Shape Dough:**
   - Shape dough into a log on a baking sheet.
4. **Bake and Slice:**
   - Bake for 20 minutes. Cool slightly, then slice into biscotti. Bake slices for 10 minutes more.

NUTRITIONAL INFORMATION (PER SERVING):

- **Calories:** 140
- **Protein:** 3g
- **Carbohydrates:** 15g
- **Fat:** 7g
- **Fiber:** 2g
- **Sodium:** 50mg

Enjoy your healthy and flavorful Honey Almond Biscotti!

Almond and Apricot Cake

Prep Time: **10 mins** | Cooking Time: **30 mins**
Yield: **8 portions**

INGREDIENTS:

- 1 cup almond flour
- 1/2 cup dried apricots, chopped
- 1/4 cup honey
- 1/4 cup olive oil
- 3 eggs
- 1 tsp baking powder
- 1 tsp vanilla extract

INSTRUCTIONS:

1. **Preheat Oven:**
   Preheat to 350°F (175°C).
2. **Mix Ingredients:**
   In a bowl, combine almond flour, apricots, honey, olive oil, eggs, baking powder, and vanilla.
3. **Bake:**
   Pour batter into a greased baking dish. Bake for 30 minutes or until golden.

NUTRITIONAL INFORMATION (PER SERVING):

- **Calories:** 220
- **Protein:** 6g
- **Carbohydrates:** 18g
- **Fat:** 14g
- **Fiber:** 3g
- **Sodium:** 60mg

Enjoy your healthy and flavorful Almond and Apricot Cake!

Orange Cardamom Cookies

Prep Time: **10 mins** | Cooking Time: **15 mins**
Yield: **12 portions**

INGREDIENTS:

- 1 cup almond flour
- 1/4 cup honey
- 1/4 cup olive oil
- 1 egg
- Zest of 1 orange
- 1 tsp ground cardamom
- 1/2 tsp baking powder

INSTRUCTIONS:

1. **Preheat Oven:**
   Preheat to 350°F (175°C).
2. **Mix Ingredients:**
   In a bowl, combine almond flour, honey, olive oil, egg, orange zest, cardamom, and baking powder.
3. **Bake:**
   Drop spoonfuls of dough onto a baking sheet. Bake for 15 minutes.

NUTRITIONAL INFORMATION (PER SERVING):

- **Calories:** 110
- **Protein:** 3g
- **Carbohydrates:** 10g
- **Fat:** 7g
- **Fiber:** 1g
- **Sodium:** 30mg

Enjoy your healthy and flavorful Orange Cardamom Cookies!

Poached Pears with Red Wine

Prep Time: **10 mins** | Cooking Time: **30 mins**
Yield: **4 portions**

INGREDIENTS:

- 4 pears, peeled
- 2 cups red wine
- 1/4 cup honey
- 1 cinnamon stick
- 2 cloves
- 1 strip orange zest

INSTRUCTIONS:

1. **Simmer:**
   - In a pot, combine wine, honey, cinnamon, cloves, and orange zest. Bring to a simmer.
2. **Poach Pears:**
   - Add pears and simmer for 30 minutes, turning occasionally.
3. **Serve:**
   - Serve warm or chilled.

NUTRITIONAL INFORMATION (PER SERVING):

- **Calories:** 150
- **Protein:** 0g
- **Carbohydrates:** 28g
- **Fat:** 0g
- **Fiber:** 4g
- **Sodium:** 5mg

Enjoy your healthy and flavorful Poached Pears with Red Wine!

Pistachio Baklava Rolls

Prep Time: **15 mins** | Cooking Time: **25 mins**
Yield: **12 portions**

INGREDIENTS:

- 1 cup pistachios, chopped
- 1/2 cup honey
- 1/4 cup olive oil
- 1 tsp cinnamon
- 8 sheets phyllo dough

INSTRUCTIONS:

1. **Preheat Oven:**
   - Preheat to 350°F (175°C).
2. **Prepare Filling:**
   - Mix pistachios, honey, olive oil, and cinnamon in a bowl.
3. **Assemble Rolls:**
   - Layer 2 sheets of phyllo, brushing with olive oil between layers. Spread filling along one edge and roll tightly. Repeat with remaining phyllo and filling.
4. **Bake:**
   - Place rolls on a baking sheet and bake for 25 minutes.

NUTRITIONAL INFORMATION (PER SERVING):

- **Calories:** 150
- **Protein:** 2g
- **Carbohydrates:** 18g
- **Fat:** 8g
- **Fiber:** 1g
- **Sodium:** 50mg

Enjoy your healthy and flavorful Pistachio Baklava Rolls!

Honey and Cinnamon Roasted Figs

Prep Time: **5 mins** | Cooking Time: **15 mins**
Yield: **4 portions**

INGREDIENTS:

- 8 fresh figs, halved
- 2 tbsp honey
- 1 tsp cinnamon
- 1 tbsp olive oil

INSTRUCTIONS:

1. **Preheat Oven:**
   - Preheat to 375°F (190°C).
2. **Prepare Figs:**
   - Place figs on a baking sheet, drizzle with honey and olive oil, and sprinkle with cinnamon.
3. **Roast:**
   - Roast for 15 minutes.

NUTRITIONAL INFORMATION (PER SERVING):

- **Calories:** 100
- **Protein:** 1g
- **Carbohydrates:** 18g
- **Fat:** 3g
- **Fiber:** 2g
- **Sodium:** 0mg

Enjoy your healthy and flavorful Honey and Cinnamon Roasted Figs!

Spiced Apple and Walnut Cake

Prep Time: **10 mins** | Cooking Time: **30 mins**
Yield: **8 portions**

INGREDIENTS:

- 1 cup whole wheat flour
- 1/2 cup walnuts, chopped
- 2 apples, peeled and grated
- 1/4 cup honey
- 1/4 cup olive oil
- 2 eggs
- 1 tsp cinnamon
- 1/2 tsp nutmeg
- 1 tsp baking powder

INSTRUCTIONS:

1. **Preheat Oven:**
   - Preheat to 350°F (175°C).
2. **Mix Ingredients:**
   - In a bowl, combine flour, walnuts, apples, honey, olive oil, eggs, cinnamon, nutmeg, and baking powder.
3. **Bake:**
   - Pour batter into a greased baking dish. Bake for 30 minutes.

NUTRITIONAL INFORMATION (PER SERVING):

- **Calories:** 200
- **Protein:** 4g
- **Carbohydrates:** 24g
- **Fat:** 10g
- **Fiber:** 3g
- **Sodium:** 60mg

Enjoy your healthy and flavorful Spiced Apple and Walnut Cake!

Fig and Ricotta Tartlets

Prep Time: **10 mins** | Cooking Time: **15 mins**
Yield: **6 portions**

INGREDIENTS:

- 6 phyllo pastry sheets
- 1 cup ricotta cheese
- 6 fresh figs, halved
- 2 tbsp honey
- 1 tsp lemon zest
- 1 tsp vanilla extract
- Olive oil spray

INSTRUCTIONS:

1. **Preheat Oven:**
   - Preheat to 375°F (190°C).
2. **Prepare Pastry:**
   - Spray phyllo sheets with olive oil and layer. Cut into 6 squares and fit into muffin tin.
3. **Fill Tartlets:**
   - Mix ricotta, lemon zest, and vanilla. Spoon into phyllo cups and top with fig halves.
4. **Bake:**
   - Bake for 15 minutes. Drizzle with honey.

NUTRITIONAL INFORMATION (PER SERVING):

- **Calories:** 150
- **Protein:** 5g
- **Carbohydrates:** 18g
- **Fat:** 7g
- **Fiber:** 1g
- **Sodium:** 100mg

Enjoy your healthy and flavorful Fig and Ricotta Tartlets!

Lemon and Almond Tart

Prep Time: **15 mins** | Cooking Time: **30 mins**
Yield: **8 portions**

INGREDIENTS:

- 1 cup almond flour
- 1/4 cup honey
- 1/4 cup olive oil
- 2 eggs
- Zest of 2 lemons
- Juice of 1 lemon
- 1 tsp baking powder

INSTRUCTIONS:

1. **Preheat Oven:**
   - Preheat to 350°F (175°C).
2. **Mix Ingredients:**
   - Combine almond flour, honey, olive oil, eggs, lemon zest, lemon juice, and baking powder in a bowl.
3. **Bake:**
   - Pour mixture into a greased tart pan. Bake for 30 minutes.

NUTRITIONAL INFORMATION (PER SERVING):

- **Calories:** 180
- **Protein:** 5g
- **Carbohydrates:** 14g
- **Fat:** 12g
- **Fiber:** 2g
- **Sodium:** 40mg

Enjoy your healthy and flavorful Lemon and Almond Tart!

Honey and Nut Stuffed Dates

Prep Time: **10 mins** | Cooking Time: **None**
Yield: **12 portions**

INGREDIENTS:

- 12 Medjool dates, pitted
- 1/4 cup mixed nuts, chopped
- 2 tbsp honey
- 1/4 tsp cinnamon (optional)

INSTRUCTIONS:

1. **Stuff Dates:**
   - Fill each date with chopped nuts.
2. **Drizzle Honey:**
   - Drizzle honey over stuffed dates.
3. **Optional:**
   - Sprinkle with cinnamon if desired.

NUTRITIONAL INFORMATION (PER SERVING):

- **Calories:** 80
- **Protein:** 1g
- **Carbohydrates:** 16g
- **Fat:** 2g
- **Fiber:** 2g
- **Sodium:** 0mg

Enjoy your healthy and flavorful Honey and Nut Stuffed Dates!

Orange and Olive Oil Muffins

Prep Time: **10 mins** | Cooking Time: **20 mins**
Yield: **12 portions**

INGREDIENTS:

- 1 1/2 cups whole wheat flour
- 1/2 cup honey
- 1/2 cup olive oil
- 2 eggs
- Zest of 2 oranges
- Juice of 1 orange
- 1 tsp baking powder
- 1/2 tsp baking soda

INSTRUCTIONS:

1. **Preheat Oven:**
   - Preheat to 350°F (175°C).
2. **Mix Wet Ingredients:**
   - In a bowl, combine honey, olive oil, eggs, orange zest, and juice.
3. **Mix Dry Ingredients:**
   - In another bowl, mix flour, baking powder, and baking soda.
4. **Combine:**
   - Gradually add dry ingredients to wet ingredients. Mix until just combined.
5. **Bake:**
   - Divide batter into a greased muffin tin. Bake for 20 minutes.

NUTRITIONAL INFORMATION (PER SERVING):

- **Calories:** 180
- **Protein:** 3g
- **Carbohydrates:** 22g
- **Fat:** 9g
- **Fiber:** 2g
- **Sodium:** 80mg

Enjoy your healthy and flavorful Orange and Olive Oil Muffins!

APPENDIX MEASUREMENT CONVERSION CHART

VOLUME EQUIVALENTS(DRY)

US STANDARD	METRIC (APPROXIMATE)
1/8 teaspoon	0.5 mL
1/4 teaspoon	1 mL
1/2 teaspoon	2 mL
3/4 teaspoon	4 mL
1 teaspoon	5 mL
1 tablespoon	15 mL
1/4 cup	59 mL
1/2 cup	118 mL
3/4 cup	177 mL
1 cup	235 mL
2 cups	475 mL
3 cups	700 mL
4 cups	1 L

WEIGHT EQUIVALENTS

US STANDARD	METRIC (APPROXIMATE)
1 ounce	28 g
2 ounces	57 g
5 ounces	142 g
10 ounces	284 g
15 ounces	425 g
16 ounces (1 pound)	455 g
	680 g
1.5 pounds	907 g

VOLUME EQUIVALENTS(LIQUID)

US STANDARD	US STANDARD (OUNCES)	METRIC (APPROXIMATE)
2 tablespoons	1 fl.oz.	30 mL
1/4 cup	2 fl.oz.	60 mL
1/2 cup	4 fl.oz.	120 mL
1 cup	8 fl.oz.	240 mL
1 1/2 cup	12 fl.oz.	355 mL
2 cups or 1 pint	16 fl.oz.	475 mL
4 cups or 1 quart	32 fl.oz.	1 L
1 gallon	128 fl.oz.	4 L

TEMPERATURES EQUIVALENTS

FAHRENHEIT(F)	CELSIUS(C) (APPROXIMATE)
225 °F	107 °C
250 °F	120 °C
275 °F	135 °C
300 °F	150 °C
325 °F	160 °C
350 °F	180 °C
375 °F	190 °C
400 °F	205 °C
425 °F	220 °C
450 °F	235 °C
475 °F	245 °C
500 °F	260 °C

APPENDIX 30-DAY MEAL PLAN

DAYS	BREAKFAST	LUNCH	DINNER	SNACK/DESERT
1	Hummus Toast with Cucumbers and Radishes	Vegetable Paella	Shrimp Scampi with Garlic and Olive Oil	Orange Blossom Semolina Cake
2	Spinach and Feta Frittata	Penne Arrabbiata with Olives	Stuffed Acorn Squash with Quinoa	Garlic Shrimp Skewers
3	Shakshuka (Poached Eggs in Tomato Sauce)	Greek Style Lentil Soup	Pasta with Anchovy Sauce	Date and Walnut Bars
4	Herbed Goat Cheese and Vegetable Muffins	Ricotta and Spinach Stuffed Manicotti	Rice and Bean Stuffed Peppers	Poached Pears with Red Wine
5	Millet Porridge with Nuts and Fruits	Pasta with Anchovy Sauce	Baked Salmon with Dill and Lemon	Spiced Apple and Walnut Cake
6	Mediterranean Breakfast Tacos	Mediterranean Veggie Pizza	Greek Salad with Feta and Olives	Honey and Nut Stuffed Dates
7	Peta and Spinach Muffins	Ratatouille	Pappardelle with Mushroom Ragu	Almond and Apricot Cake
8	Whole Wheat Pancakes with Fresh Berries	Bulgur Wheat Salad	Mediterranean Vegetable Stir-Fry	Spanakopita Triangles
9	Mediterranean Breakfast Bowl	Greek Lemon Chicken	Caprese Pasta with Fresh Basil	Lemon and Herb Marinated Feta
10	Avocado Toast with Cherry Tomatoes	Braised Lamb with Apricots	Garlic Butter Shrimp with Zoodles	Saffron Rice Pudding
11	Millet Porridge with Nuts and Fruits	Zucchini Noodles with Marinara	Chickpea Pasta with Garlic and Parsley	Feta Stuffed Dates
12	Mediterranean Smoothie Bowl	Beef and Mushroom Stew	Lamb Gyro	Pistachio Baklava Rolls
13	Shakshuka (Poached Eggs in Tomato Sauce)	Herbed Turkey Meatloaf	Roasted Beet and Goat Cheese Sandwich	Greek Yogurt Dip with Fresh Veggies
14	Mediterranean Omelette with Sun-Dried Tomatoes	Baked Salmon with Dill and Lemon	Grilled Swordfish with Capers	Fig and Ricotta Tartlets
15	Lemon Ricotta Pancakes	Chickpea and Vegetable Tagine	Grilled Calamari with Lemon and Parsley	Falafel with Tzatziki

DAYS	BREAKFAST	LUNCH	DINNER	SNACK/DESERT
16	Shrimp and Avocado Sandwich	Greek Style Stuffed Zucchini	Caprese Pasta with Fresh Basil	Marinated Olives
17	Egg and Veggie Breakfast Wrap	Seafood Risotto with Saffron	Greek Style Stuffed Zucchini	Zucchini Fritters
18	Mediterranean Breakfast Tacos	Beef and Eggplant Casserole	Roasted Eggplant with Tahini	Cheese and Olive Platter
19	Quinoa Breakfast Porridge	Tofu and Vegetable Stir-Fry	Grilled Octopus with Lemon and Olive Oil	Feta Stuffed Dates
20	Tofu Scramble with Mediterranean Veggies	Red Lentil Soup with Lemon	Three-Bean Salad with Lemon Vinaigrette	Honey and Cinnamon Roasted Figs
21	Whole Wheat Pancakes with Fresh Berries	Lemon and Artichoke Penne	Penne Arrabbiata with Olives	Greek Yogurt with Honey and Walnuts
22	Avocado Toast with Cherry Tomatoes	Black Bean and Corn Salad	Grilled Shrimp with Mango Salsa	Mediterranean Bruschetta
23	Hummus Toast with Cucumbers and Radishes	Mediterranean Bulgur Pilaf	Pan-Seared Scallops with Herb Butter	Roasted Eggplant Dip
24	Mediterranean Breakfast Bowl	Spinach and Ricotta Stuffed Peppers	Baked Tilapia with Spinach and Feta	Lemon and Almond Tart
25	Shakshuka (Poached Eggs in Tomato Sauce)	Spinach and Feta Flatbread	Chicken and Vegetable Skewers	Orange Cardamom Cookies
26	Breakfast Couscous with Honey and Nuts	Pesto and Sun-Dried Tomato Penne	Lamb Kebabs with Mint Yogurt Sauce	Hummus with Pita Chips
27	Herbed Goat Cheese and Vegetable Muffins	Spaghetti Aglio e Olio	Seared Tuna with Sesame and Soy	Honey Almond Biscotti
28	Millet Porridge with Nuts and Fruits	Grilled Chicken with Avocado Salsa	Mediterranean Mussels in White Wine Sauce	Stuffed Grape Leaves
29	Spinach and Feta Frittata	White Bean and Tuna Salad	Seafood Risotto with Saffron	Orange and Olive Oil Muffins
30	Tomato and Basil Scramble	Roasted Garlic and Herb Cauliflower Steaks	Stuffed Peppers with Ground Turkey	Pita Chips with Lemon Garlic Hummus

APPENDIX RECIPES INDEX

A.

Almond and Apricot Cake 98
Artichoke and Olive Tapenade 95
Avocado and Shrimp Salad 21
Avocado Toast with Cherry Tomatoes 10

B.

Baked Feta with Tomatoes and Olives 44
Baked Salmon with Dill and Lemon 36
Baked Stuffed Eggplant Rolls 49
Baked Tilapia with Spinach and Feta 40
Baked Zucchini Chips 47
Beef and Eggplant Casserole 31
Beef and Mushroom Stew 30
Beef and Mushroom Stroganoff 35
Beet and Orange Salad with Goat Cheese 20
Black Bean and Corn Salad 88
Braised Lamb with Apricots 27
Brown Rice Pilaf with Vegetables 87
Bulgur Wheat Salad 87

C.

Caprese Pasta with Fresh Basil 72
Caprese Salad with Balsamic Reduction 24
Caprese Sandwich 75
Cheese and Olive Platter 65
Chicken and Artichoke Casserole 33
Chicken and Vegetable Skewers 33
Chicken Cacciatore 29
Chicken Shawarma with Tahini Sauce 28
Chicken Tagine with Olives and Lemons 29
Chickpea and Spinach Curry 85
Chickpea and Spinach Stew 51
Chickpea and Vegetable Tagine 56
Chickpea Pasta with Garlic and Parsley 72
Chimichurri Sauce 94
Cucumber and Tomato Salad with Feta 25

D.

Date and Walnut Bars 97

E.

Egg and Veggie Breakfast Wrap 16
Eggplant and Tomato Bake 55
Eggplant Parmesan 50

F.

Falafel Pita 76
Falafel with Tzatziki 59
Farro Salad with Roasted Vegetables 85
Fennel and Orange Salad 26
Feta and Spinach Muffins 16
Feta Stuffed Dates 60
Fettuccine with Roasted Tomatoes 69
Fig and Ricotta Tartlets 101

G.

Garlic Butter Shrimp with Zoodles 37
Garlic Shrimp Skewers 62
Greek Gyro Wraps 74
Greek Lemon Chicken 32
Greek Salad Pizza 78
Greek Salad with Feta and Olives 19
Greek Style Lentil Soup 53
Greek Style Stuffed Shells 67
Greek Style Stuffed Zucchini 56
Greek Yogurt Dip with Fresh Veggies 64
Greek Yogurt with Honey and Walnuts 96
Grilled Asparagus with Parmesan 45
Grilled Calamari with Lemon and Parsley 42
Grilled Chicken Pesto Panini 76
Grilled Chicken with Avocado Salsa 34
Grilled Halloumi Wrap 80
Grilled Mackerel with Citrus Salsa 41
Grilled Octopus with Lemon and Olive Oil 38
Grilled Shrimp with Mango Salsa 40

H

Grilled Swordfish with Capers 37
Grilled Vegetable Skewers 55
Grilled Zucchini with Lemon and Basil 43

H

Harissa Paste 92
Herbed Goat Cheese and Vegetable Muffins .. 15
Herbed Turkey Meatloaf 30
Honey Almond Biscotti 97
Honey and Cinnamon Roasted Figs 100
Honey and Nut Stuffed Dates 102
Honey Mustard Chicken Thighs 34
Hummus and Roasted Red Pepper Sandwich .. 82
Hummus and Veggie Wraps 75
Hummus Toast with Cucumbers
and Radishes 13
Hummus with Pita Chips 58

I

Italian Sub with Olive Tapenade 81

K

Kale Salad with Lemon and Garlic 22

L

Lamb Gyro 80
Lamb Kebabs with Mint Yogurt Sauce 32
Lamb Kofta 35
Lemon and Almond Tart 101
Lemon and Artichoke Penne 66
Lemon and Garlic Shrimp Pasta 68
Lemon and Herb Marinated Feta 61
Lemon Ricotta Pancakes 15
Lentil and Vegetable Shepherd's Pie 52
Lentil and Vegetable Stew 84

M

Marinated Olives 59
Mediterranean Barley Risotto 86
Mediterranean Beef and Lentil Stew 31
Mediterranean Breakfast Bowl 11

Mediterranean Breakfast Tacos 14
Mediterranean Bruschetta 60
Mediterranean Bulgur Pilaf 91
Mediterranean Chickpea Salad 18
Mediterranean Herb Blend 93
Mediterranean Mashed Potatoes 45
Mediterranean Meatballs in Tomato Sauce ... 27
Mediterranean Mussels in White Wine Sauce .. 38
Mediterranean Omelette
with Sun-Dried Tomatoes 12
Mediterranean Quinoa Stuffed Tomatoes 47
Mediterranean Smoothie Bowl 14
Mediterranean Spelt Salad 89
Mediterranean Tuna Wrap 77
Mediterranean Turkey Club 82
Mediterranean Vegetable Casserole 54
Mediterranean Vegetable Stir-Fry 51
Mediterranean Veggie Pizza 74
Millet Porridge with Nuts and Fruits 17
Mint Yogurt Sauce 93

O

Orange and Olive Oil Muffins 102
Orange Blossom Semolina Cake 96
Orange Cardamom Cookies 98
Orzo Salad with Kalamata Olives 26

P

Pan-Seared Scallops with Herb Butter 39
Pappardelle with Mushroom Ragu 73
Pasta with Anchovy Sauce 68
Penne Arrabbiata with Olives 69
Pesto and Sun-Dried Tomato Penne 71
Pistachio Baklava Rolls 99
Pita Chips with Lemon Garlic Hummus 65
Poached Pears with Red Wine 99
Portobello Mushroom Burger 83

Q

Quinoa and Black Bean Salad 24
Quinoa Breakfast Porridge 12
Quinoa Tabbouleh 84

R

Ratatouille 44
Red Lentil and Spinach Dhal 90
Red Lentil Soup with Lemon 88
Red Wine Vinaigrette 94
Rice and Bean Stuffed Peppers 91
Ricotta and Spinach Stuffed Manicotti 71
Roasted Beet and Goat Cheese Sandwich 81
Roasted Beet Salad with Feta 48
Roasted Butternut Squash with Sage 46
Roasted Cauliflower and Chickpea Salad 25
Roasted Eggplant Dip 64
Roasted Eggplant with Tahini 43
Roasted Fennel with Parmesan 49
Roasted Garlic and Herb Cauliflower Steaks 57
Roasted Red Pepper and Chickpea Salad 21
Roasted Sea Bass with Olives and Tomatoes 42
Roasted Veggie Pita 78

S

Seafood Risotto with Saffron 39
Seared Tuna with Sesame and Soy 41
Shakshuka (Poached Eggs in Tomato Sauce) 10
Shrimp and Avocado Sandwich 77
Shrimp and Feta Linguine 67
Shrimp Scampi with Garlic and Olive Oil 36
Smoked Salmon Bagel with Cream Cheese 83
Smoked Salmon Crostini 63
Spaghetti Aglio e Olio 66
Spanakopita Triangles 58
Spiced Apple and Walnut Cake 100
Spinach and Feta Flatbread 79
Spinach and Feta Frittata 11
Spinach and Ricotta Stuffed Peppers 50
Spinach Salad with Pomegranate
and Walnuts 18
Stuffed Acorn Squash with Quinoa 52
Stuffed Acorn Squash with Wild Rice 48
Stuffed Grape Leaves 62
Stuffed Mushrooms with Spinach and Feta 46
Stuffed Peppers with Ground Turkey 28
Sun-Dried Tomato and Basil Spread 95
Sun-Dried Tomato Tapenade 63
Sweet Potato and Black Bean Enchiladas 54

T

Tabbouleh with Fresh Herbs and Lemon 19
Three-Bean Salad with Lemon Vinaigrette 90
Tofu and Vegetable Stir-Fry 57
Tofu Scramble with Mediterranean Veggies 17
Tomato and Basil Penne 70
Tomato and Mozzarella Salad with Basil 22
Turkey and Hummus Wrap 79
Tzatziki Sauce 92

V

Vegetable Paella 53

W

Warm Farro Salad with Roasted Vegetables 20
White Bean and Kale Soup 86
White Bean and Spinach Stew 89
White Bean and Tuna Salad 23
Whole Wheat Pancakes with Fresh Berries 13
Whole Wheat Spaghetti with Clams 70

Z

Zucchini Fritters 61
Zucchini Noodle Salad with Pesto 23
Zucchini Noodles with Marinara 73

Made in the USA
Columbia, SC
14 August 2024